Speaking of Values
Conversation and Listening

Irene E. Schoenberg

Longman

Speaking of Values
Conversation and Listening

Pearson Education, 10 Bank Street, White Plains, NY 10606

Acquisitions editor: Virginia Blanford
Development director: Penny Laporte
Development editors: Deborah Lazarus, Stacey Hunter
Vice president, director of design and production: Rhea Banker
Associate director of electronic production: Aliza Greenblatt
Executive managing editor: Linda Moser
Production manager: Ray Keating
Senior production editor: Robert Ruvo
Director of manufacturing: Patrice Fraccio
Senior manufacturing buyer: Edith Pullman
Art director: Patricia Wosczyk
Photo research: Tara Maldonado
Cover/interior design: Patricia Wosczyk
Associate digital layout manager: Paula D. Williams
Cover/interior illustrations: Susan Detrich
Text font: Minion
Text credits and photo credits: See p. viii.

ISBN 0-13-097881-7
ISBN 0-13-117226-3 (with Audio CD)

2 3 4 5 6 7 8 9 10 – BAH – 07 06 05 04 03

CONTENTS

SCOPE AND SEQUENCE

Unit	Listening	Pronunciation	
1 Good Neighbors	Asking for favors	Schwa /ə/	
2 Honesty	Making an excuse	Past tense endings /t/, /d/, /ɪd/	
3 Love and Marriage	A blind date	Linking /d/, /t/ and /y/	
4 The Golden Years	Super Survivors (centenarians)	Syllables and word stress	
5 Borrowing and Lending	Lending an apartment to friends	Contraction of *will*	
6 Say the Right Thing	An embarrassing situation	3rd person singular present tense endings: /s/, /z/, /ɪz/	
7 Dress for Success	A fashion show	Word stress for numbers (15 vs. 50)	
8 Medical Questions	Scientific research on genes	Stress: nouns and verbs (**pro**duce/pro**duce**)	
9 Money	Credit cards and teens	Intonation: questions and statements	
10 Sports	Parental pressure and sports	*can / can't*	
11 Pets	Pets not allowed	*walk / work* *won't / want*	
12 The Right Gift	Regifting	Word stress and meaning	

From the News	Act It Out	Beyond the Classroom
Ugly Houses Not Allowed	Making and responding to suggestions	Describing a neighbor
Bad News for Liars	Asking about and expressing likes and dislikes	Telling a folktale about honesty
Books to Test True Love	Asking about and expressing preferences	Finding out about wedding customs around the world
Forced Retirement in Canada Is a Dinosaur	Asking for suggestions/Giving advice/Explaining consequences	Telling a folktale about older people
Be Careful When Lending to Relatives	Making formal introductions/Stating or asking about a business purpose	Opening a bank account
Remembering Names	Confirming information/Contradicting someone	Understanding cross-cultural differences
Your Image at Work	Making and resolving a complaint	Describing unusual outfits
Sleep-Deprived Teens Run Risk of Depression	Asking about and describing a medical problem/Suggesting a remedy	Finding out about alternative medicines
Young Spenders	Presenting someone with something/Expressing thanks	Ranking salaries of different professions
Helping Young Golfer with True Handicap	Giving and clarifying instructions	Finding out about famous athletes
San Francisco Citizens to Become "Pet Guardians"	Raising and countering objectives	Caring for an unusual pet
Giving Gifts Around the World	Making and rejecting suggestions	Choosing gifts from catalogs

PREFACE

Speaking of Values is aimed at encouraging intermediate students to address and discuss different real-life problems. For example:

- *You're in your apartment, and you hear loud crying. You think the woman next door is hitting her children and hurting them. What do you do?*

- *You're taking a final exam. Your good friend wants to see your answers. You want to help him out, but you don't want to get into trouble. What do you do?*

- *Your nephew has introduced you to his fiancée. She's twice his age. What do you say?*

- *You're late for a job interview when you notice a button is missing from your suit. What do you do?*

Such issues encourage students to compare their ideas and values with those of classmates with other backgrounds, personalities, and cultures. Because there are no right or wrong answers to these questions, students lose their fear of being wrong and concentrate on using English to discuss ideas and develop critical thinking skills.

In the past decade, new ideas have emerged about language teaching. While we still acknowledge the benefits of interactive activities based on motivating content, we also realize the value of systematically incorporating language-focused exercises. Beyond the basic level, the difference between the weaker and stronger student is often a difference of lexical ability. Stronger students appear more fluent because they have a greater variety of phrases at the tips of their tongues. And the most efficient way to develop this fluency is by selecting and focusing on expressions and phrases in context and then practicing them in meaningful and enjoyable ways.

In addition, there has been an increased emphasis on listening comprehension skills, not just as an aid to better speaking but also as a way of understanding language that is more complex than the language a student can produce. For some people, understanding English is a goal in itself.

Speaking of Values incorporates these ideas by including a lexical segment and a complete listening component.

Each unit of *Speaking of Values* contains the following sections:

THINK ABOUT THE TOPIC

Illustrations or photos followed by questions whet students' interest in and activate their knowledge of the unit subject.

TALK ABOUT YOUR EXPERIENCE

In Part A, students answer a set of questions based on personal experience and then ask a classmate the same questions. The discussion questions that follow in Part B are more open-ended, drawing from and building on the questions in Part A.

LISTENING

Each listening task involves an issue that relates to the unit subject. For example, Unit 1, Good Neighbors, raises the question of what to do if a neighbor asks for too many favors. Unit 2, Honesty, involves a person caught telling a lie to a friend.

Warm-up questions prepare the class for what they will hear. Comprehension questions follow each listening, and opinion questions end this section.

PRONUNCIATION

Students focus on a few sentences from the Listening and learn about a common feature of English pronunciation such as stress, intonation, or verb endings.

PROBLEM SOLVING

Problem Solving still remains at the heart of the text. Students consider problems that are difficult to answer because there are two sides to the question. They read or listen to the problem. They choose a solution and explain their reasons orally or in writing. Then, working in small groups, they must come to an agreement on a solution.

In this edition, the problems are recorded, giving the teacher more options in using the material. Students can listen with their books closed. Students can listen, write the problem, and check what they've written by comparing their version to the one in the book. Students can listen to the problem and choose a possible solution before looking at the choices in the book.

FROM THE NEWS

Students read summaries of authentic news articles. Follow-up questions help students practice comprehension of main ideas, words and phrases from context, and inference. A final question asks students to express their opinion.

WORDS AND PHRASES

Students learn words and phrases related to the topic or that have come directly from the Problem Solving or In the News sections. Short quizzes based on the words and phrases from each unit are included in the Teacher's Pack, and can be photocopied for classroom use.

ACT IT OUT

Students do a role-play that relates to the unit's theme, learning useful functions such as making suggestions, expressing likes and dislikes, giving advice, and explaining consequences. Unlike many of the other sections of the book, here students do not have to express their opinions. Rather, they become actors who learn parts and improvise in any way they wish.

PROVERBS

Students read and talk about proverbs related to the theme. They are encouraged to give examples that illustrate their meanings and to share similar proverbs from their own cultures.

BEYOND THE CLASSROOM

A homework assignment asks students to bring to class information they've gathered from the Internet, the library, people outside the class, or other sources and report to the class. Motivated students can produce amazing results and become an inspiration to others.

APPENDIX
The appendix contains an index of the vocabulary and functions presented and practiced in the text.

AUDIOCASSETTE AND CD

The Listening, Pronunciation, Problem Solving and From the News sections have been recorded on cassettes and CDs. The symbol ⌒ appears next to these activities. Tapescripts for recorded material that does not appear in the text can be found in the Teacher's Pack.

TEACHER'S PACK

A separate Teacher's Pack includes the student book answer key, teaching suggestions for each section, quizzes for each unit, the answer key for the quizzes, and tapescripts for the Listening and Pronunciation sections.

TEXT CREDITS

Page 7, "Ugly Houses Not Allowed" based on an original article in *The New York Times*, July 13, 2000 as it appeared in Lexis Nexis. **Page 18**, "Bad News for Liars" based on an original article in *The Chicago-Sun Times*, November 29, 2000 as it appeared in Lexis Nexis. **Page 27**, "Books to Test True Love" based on an original article in *The New York Times* by Arnold Martin, September 20, 2000 as it appeared in Lexis Nexis. **Page 37**, "Forced Retirement in Canada is a Dinosaur" based on an original article in *The Toronto Star*, July 15, 2000, Saturday Edition 1 as it appeared in Lexis Nexis. **Page 46**, "Be Careful When Lending to Relatives" based on an original article in *The Baltimore Sun* by Eileen Ambrose, September 17, 2000 as it appeared in Lexis Nexis. **Page 56**, "Remembering Names" based on an original article in *The Guardian*, London, June 22, 2000 as it appeared in Lexis Nexis. **Page 65**, "Your Image at Work" based on an original article in *The Independent*, London, November 19, 2000 as it appeared in Lexis Nexis. **Page 76**, "Sleep-Deprived Teens Run Risk of Depression" based on an original article in *The Toronto Sun*, March 11, 2001 as it appeared in Lexis Nexis. **Page 85**, "Young Spenders" based on an original article in *The Irish Times*, May 2, 2001, City Edition as it appeared in Lexis Nexis. **Page 95**, "Helping Young Golfer with True Handicap" based on an original article in *The Tampa Tribune*, June 15, 2001 as it appeared in Lexis Nexis. **Page 114**, "Giving Gifts around the World" based on an original article in *The Pittsburgh Post-Gazette*, December 17, 2000 as it appeared in Lexis Nexis.

PHOTO CREDITS

Page 21 ©ImageState-Pictor/ImageState-Pictor/PictureQuest.
Page 32 top: ©Earl & Nazima Kowall/CORBIS.
Page 32 bottom left: ©EyeWire Collection/Getty Images.
Page 32 bottom right: ©Rob Cage/Getty Images/Taxi.
Page 80 ©William Whitehurst/CORBIS.
Page 90 left: ©EyeWire Collection/Getty Images.
Page 90 top right: ©AP/Wide World Photos/Joan C. Fahrenthold.
Page 90 bottom right: ©PhotoLink/Getty Images.

ACKNOWLEDGMENTS

The author would like to thank the following:

- My friends, colleagues, and students at the International English Language Institute of Hunter College

- At Longman: Eleanor Barnes, Louisa Hellegers, Penny Laporte, Ginny Blanford, Debbie Lazarus-Yargazaway, Stacey Hunter, and Robert Ruvo

- The following reviewers: Cynthia Wiseman, LaGuardia Community College, Hunter College, and John Jay College, New York; Diane Mahin, University of Miami, Florida; Randy Schafer, various programs, Japan; Christina Cavage, Atlantic Cape Community College, New Jersey; Linda Wells, University of Washington; Linda Pelc, LaGuardia Community College, New York; Robert Teare, Osaka Institute of Technology, Kinki University and Osaka Geidai Tandai, Japan; Susan Stempleski, Hunter College, New York.

Good Neighbors

THINK ABOUT THE TOPIC

1. What's happening in each apartment in the picture?
2. Do you have any neighbors like the ones in the picture? Explain.

TALK ABOUT YOUR EXPERIENCE

A *Answer the questions. Then ask a classmate.*

	You	Your Classmate
1. Where do you live? In an apartment? In a private house? In a dormitory?		
2. Do your neighbors have pets? Do they play instruments? Do they listen to loud music?		
3. What do you know about your next-door neighbor? Do you know his or her name? Occupation? Interests?		
4. How many times have you been inside your neighbor's home?		

B *Discuss with the class.*

1. What did you learn about your classmate's neighbors? Tell the class.
2. What kind of neighbor are you?
3. Do you think neighbors are warmer and more helpful in the countryside than in the city? Are they warmer and more helpful in the suburbs than in the city? Are neighbors more helpful in some countries than in others? Explain.

LISTENING

A *Answer the questions before you listen.*

1. What would you feel comfortable asking a neighbor to do for you?
2. Have you done these favors for a neighbor—fed a pet, watered plants, picked up the mail?

B *Listen to the conversation between two neighbors. Then read the chart. Listen again. Check (✓) what Mrs. Grant asks and what Kate agrees to do.*

	Mrs. Grant asks Kate to	Kate agrees to
mail some letters		
get her mail		
plant some flowers		
water some plants		
take care of her frog		
take care of her dog		

C *Complete the sentences. Then discuss your opinions with a partner.*

1. In my opinion, Kate was _____.

   a. rude   **b.** polite   **c.** too nice

2. In my opinion, Mrs. Grant's requests were _____.

   a. reasonable   **b.** unreasonable   **c.** reasonable for neighbors

PRONUNCIATION

A *Listen to these sentences.*

- Have **a** nice day.
- I've got **a** lot **of** work.

The words *a* and *of* aren't stressed. They are pronounced with a schwa sound. The schwa /ə/ is the most common vowel sound in spoken English. It's used in unstressed syllables when people speak quickly. It's the sound of "uh."

B *Now listen to these sentences. Put a check (✓) above those underlined words that have a schwa sound. Check your answers on page 9.*

1. It seems <u>to</u> <u>be</u> coming later and later.
2. I have <u>a</u> couple <u>of</u> little favors <u>to</u> ask.
3. <u>Do</u> you have <u>a</u> lot <u>of</u> plants?

C *Listen again and repeat each sentence.*

WORDS AND PHRASES

A *Work with a partner. Complete the conversations with a word from the box. Check your dictionary for any new words. Then read the conversations out loud.*

clean	lazy	quiet	industrious	selfish
noisy	rude	~~dirty~~	thoughtful	

1. A: My neighbor never cleans his apartment, and he takes out the garbage only once a week.

   B: Sounds like your neighbor is very _____dirty_____.

2. A: My neighbor drives the older people in our building to the supermarket and gets them groceries when they're sick.

   B: Sounds like you have a very _____ neighbor.

3. A: My neighbor sits around and watches TV all day long. He doesn't work or study.

   B: Sounds like your neighbor is very _____.

4. A: No matter what you do for him, my neighbor never says "thank you."

   B: Sounds like you have a very _____ neighbor.

5. A: My neighbor listens to loud music almost all day long. When he isn't listening to music, he's playing the drums.

   B: Sounds like your neighbor is very _____.

6. A: My neighbor never thinks of others, only of himself.

   B: Sounds like you have a very _____ neighbor.

7. A: My neighbor is a nurse during the day. She teaches nursing one night a week and attends school one night a week.

   B: Sounds like your neighbor is very _____.

8. A: My neighbor's home is spotless.

   B: Sounds like you have a very _____ neighbor.

9. A: I never hear my neighbor.

   B: Sounds like your neighbor is very _____.

B *Write three qualities you think are important in a good neighbor.*

1. _____

2. _____

3. _____

Compare with a partner. Explain why you chose those qualities.

C *Look at the picture on page 1. Describe the people and apartments using the words from the box in Part A.*

> **EXAMPLES**
>
> *Apartment 7C is clean.*
> *The people in 8C are noisy.*

D *Complete the conversation with the idioms from the box. Part of the expression may already be in the conversation. Then practice the conversation with a partner.*

a cold fish	blow hot and cold
a good Samaritan	be down to earth
a busybody	

A: Hi, hon. How come you're home so late?

B: Our next-door neighbor asked me all sorts of personal questions and then talked about everyone on this block.

A: Sorry to hear that. He sounds like a _____. Have you met
   the woman across the street?
            1

B: Yes, a few times. She blows _____ and _____.
                   2   **3**
   One day she's warm and friendly. The next time she's a _____
                                                 4
   fish.

A: I spoke to her once. I think she's a snob.

B: Well, the guy two houses down isn't a snob. He's very friendly.

A: He's also very down _____ and helpful. The other day I was
                           5
   trying to fix Dad's wheelchair. He stopped painting his house and
   helped me. It took us almost two hours.

B: What a good _____!
                 6

E *Match the idioms on the left with their definitions on the right. Write the correct letter on the line.*

_____ **1.** blow hot and cold

_____ **2.** down to earth

_____ **3.** a cold fish

_____ **4.** a busybody

_____ **5.** a good Samaritan

a. unfriendly

b. someone who wants to know about other people's personal lives

c. practical, direct, and sensible

d. someone who helps others with problems

e. keep changing your behavior toward someone

PROBLEM SOLVING

A *Read and listen to each problem. Choose a solution and write your reason for choosing that solution.*

Problem 1

Your inconsiderate neighbor practices the piano every day from two in the afternoon until midnight. Several times you've asked him not to practice at night. Each time, he stops practicing for two or three nights, but then he starts again. You're a student. You study best in a quiet place.

You:

a. buy earplugs.

b. write a letter to your landlord.

c. complain to the police.

d. move.

e. other: _____

Reason: _____

Problem 2

You're in your apartment, and you hear loud crying. You think the woman next door is hitting one of her children and hurting the child.

You:

a. mind your own business.

b. bang on the wall.

c. visit the family.

d. call the police.

e. other: _____

Reason: _____

You moved to a new home four months ago. The woman next door was very helpful when you moved in. You were grateful and invited her to dinner. Soon she began dropping in right after dinner and staying for about two hours. At first you thought it was nice. Now she visits every evening and asks all sorts of personal questions.

You:

a. pretend not to be home.

b. open the door and tell her you're busy.

c. tell her exactly how you feel.

d. begin visiting her every night.

e. other: _____

Reason: _____

B *Work in small groups. Talk about each problem in Part A and decide what your group would do.*

FROM THE NEWS

A *Look at the picture. What's wrong with the house in the picture? Read and listen to the article.*

UGLY HOUSES NOT ALLOWED

Many cities have laws against air, water, and noise pollution. Portland, Oregon has a law against a different kind of pollution— "visual" pollution. The city government of Portland believes ugly houses are a form of visual pollution, so the law states that at least 15 percent of the front of new houses must be windows and doors. Also, you cannot build a house whose garage takes up more than half the front of the house.

B *Answer the questions.*

1. What are four kinds of pollution?

2. Where is there a law against visual pollution?

3. What does the law say you can and can't do?

C *Read the opinions of these people.*

Person A: I think the law is terrible. If I buy a house, I want to do what I want with my home. I believe my home is my castle.

Person B: I disagree. I think the law is good. I want to have an attractive neighborhood. An ugly home lowers the value of all the houses. I don't want people to build houses without windows.

Person C: I don't think windows are beautiful. Beauty is in the eyes of the beholder.

Person D: In my opinion, some people may need a garage more than they need windows.

D *Discuss your opinion with the class. Use the expressions in the box to help you.*

EXPRESSING OPINIONS	
I think . . .	I agree . . .
I don't think . . .	I don't agree . . .
I believe . . .	In my opinion . . .
I don't believe . . .	

ACT IT OUT

Act out the situation with a partner. Use the language from the box.

MAKING SUGGESTIONS		RESPONDING TO SUGGESTIONS
Why don't you	*tell her you're busy?* *pretend to be out?*	That's a good idea. I don't think that would work.
You could . . .		
You may want to . . .		

Situation

A: You have one of the problems listed at the top of page 9. Tell **B** about the problem. Include as many details as you can.

B: Listen to **A's** problem. Ask questions about the problem. Suggest different ways to solve it. Decide on a solution together.

Problems

1. Your neighbor is noisy.
2. Your neighbor is a busybody.
3. Your neighbor blows hot and cold.
4. Your neighbor may be hurting his or her child.

PROVERBS

Work in small groups. Discuss what these sayings mean. Do you agree ?

> ◆ *Good fences make good neighbors.*
> —Robert Frost, "Mending Wall"
>
> ◆ *No one is rich enough to do without a neighbor.*
> —Danish proverb
>
> ◆ *Do not judge your neighbor until you walk two moons in his moccasins.*
> —Native American proverb

BEYOND THE CLASSROOM

Tell about your neighbor. Or tell about yourself as your neighbor sees you.

- Use three words to describe this person.
- Let the class decide if you are describing your neighbor or yourself.

The class listens and takes notes. Each student writes about three of the people.

> **EXAMPLE**
>
> *"This person is friendly. She always greets people in the elevator. She's also very busy. She works six days a week and sometimes comes home after nine. She never walks. She always runs. Her apartment is beautiful. It's clean and sunny. She has many beautiful plants in it. She's helpful and a wonderful neighbor."*

Answers to Pronunciation B, page 3:

1. It seems to be coming later and later.
2. I have a couple of little favors to ask.
3. Do you have a lot of plants?

Honesty

THINK ABOUT THE TOPIC

1. If you were the people in these drawings, what would you say or do?
2. Which people are being honest?

TALK ABOUT YOUR EXPERIENCE

A *Answer the questions. Then ask a classmate.*

1. Have you ever said you were:
    a. sick when you were not sick?
    b. busy when you were not busy?
    c. older or younger than you were?

2. Have you ever cheated on:
    a. a test?
    b. the train, bus, or subway fare?
    c. the speed limit?
    d. a job application?

3. Have you ever copied:
    a. a CD or cassette tape?
    b. a book?
    c. a videotape?
    d. a computer program or game?

4. Have you ever lied to a good friend?

5. Do you know anyone who has taken something small from:
    a. a hotel? (ashtrays, towels, etc.)
    b. his or her office? (pens, pencils, paper)

B *Discuss with the class.*

1. In what situations do you think it's OK to:
    a. lie to a friend?
    b. take something that doesn't belong to you?
    c. make a copy of something?

2. When you discover someone has lied to you, do you feel angry? hurt? sad? Explain.

LISTENING

A *Answer the question before you listen.*

You are invited to a party, but you don't want to go. Would you give either of these excuses?

- "Sorry I can't come to your party. I'm working late."
- "Sorry, I really don't enjoy parties much, but I'd love to see you some other time."

B *Listen to the conversation. Read the questions. Listen again. Then check (✓) all the correct answers to the questions.*

1. Where was John last night?

   _____ **a.** He was working late at the office.

   _____ **b.** He was working at home.

   _____ **c.** He was at the movies.

   _____ **d.** He was with Cindy.

   _____ **e.** He went out for something to eat.

2. What was true at the end of the conversation?

   _____ **a.** John knows that he acted badly.

   _____ **b.** Sarah is angry at John.

   _____ **c.** John apologizes.

   _____ **d.** John is angry at Sarah.

   _____ **e.** Sarah is understanding.

   _____ **f.** John is sorry he made an excuse.

C *Discuss with the class.*

1. If you were John's friend, Sarah, how would you feel?
2. Would you continue to be John's friend? Explain.

PRONUNCIATION

Regular verbs in the past tense end in *-ed* but have three different final sounds: /t/, /d/, /ɪd/.

| | /t/ | /d/ | /ɪd/ |
| talked | tried | wanted |

🎧 **B** *Listen to each sentence and repeat. Write the main verb on the line next to the number. Then check (✓) the column of the past tense ending you hear. Check your answers on page 20.*

Verb	/t/	/d/	/ɪd/
1. missed	✓		
2.			
3.			
4.			
5.			
6.			

WORDS AND PHRASES I

A *Complete the conversation with phrases from the box. Part of the phrase may already be in the conversation. Then practice the conversation with a partner.*

A: Are you going to the meeting?

B: Yes, but I'd really like to get _____ of it.
     1

A: Me, too. I _____ stand Dino. He's bossy and boring.
     2

B: Maybe he won't show _____ .
     3

A: No _____ luck. He never misses a meeting.
     4

B: Listen. Let's say we have another meeting.

A: We can't. That's a bald- _____ lie.
     5

B: Well, then, let's have a meeting. In my office.
     You and me. Three o'clock.

A: Perfect. Now it's just a little white lie.

> no such luck = we won't be so lucky
>
> get out of = not have to do
>
> bald-faced lie = a clear lie
>
> show up = appear
>
> can't stand = dislike

B *Rewrite these sentences. Use an expression from the box in Part A.*

1. I wish I didn't have to write that report.

   <u>I wish I could get out of writing that report.</u>

2. I really don't like attending meetings.

   _____

3. The director didn't come until noon.

   _____

4. We won't be so lucky. We have to do that report.

   _____

5. It was a big lie. He didn't write the paper by himself. He had a lot of help.

   _____

C *Work with a partner. Write the phrase from the box next to its definition. Use a dictionary if necessary.*

tell a white lie	have an alibi	make a suggestion
make an excuse	state a fact	make a decision
tell a tall tale	give an opinion	~~make a mistake~~

1. do something incorrectly = <u>make a mistake</u>

2. give a false reason for not doing something = _____

3. come up with an idea for something = _____

4. explain why you couldn't have committed a crime = _____

5. make a choice after discussion or thought = _____

6. tell a small lie = _____

7. tell an unbelievable story = _____

8. give true information = _____

9. give your own thoughts about something = _____

D *Read each conversation on the next page. Then answer the questions. Use the phrases from Part C.*

| Policeman: | A man was killed on this street last night. Where were you between 8:00 and 10:00 p.m. last night? |
| Man: | I was visiting my brother in Connecticut. |

1. What did the man have?   <u>He had an alibi.</u>

| Mother: | Where are all the cookies? |
| Child: | A monster came and ate them. |

2. What did the child do?   _____

| Teacher: | At what temperature does water boil? |
| Student: | Water boils at 100° Celsius or 212° Fahrenheit. |

3. What did the student do?   _____

| Woman: | That painting is beautiful. |
| Man: | Really? I'm not crazy about it. |

4. What did both the woman and man do?   _____

| Teacher: | What's sixty-three divided by nine? |
| Student: | Eight. |

5. What did the student do?   _____

| Woman: | What do you think of my new hairdo? |
| Friend: | (doesn't like the hairdo) It's . . . it's . . . uh . . . it's nice. |

6. What did the friend do?   _____

| Husband: | It's a beautiful day. Why don't we take a walk? |
| Wife: | Good idea. |

7. What did the husband do?   _____

| Man: | I've finally decided to quit my job and start my own business. |
| Woman: | That's wonderful. Lots of luck. |

8. What did the man do?   _____

(continued on next page)

Student: Sorry I'm late. I missed my train.

Woman: Try to be on time.

9. What did the student do? _____

PROBLEM SOLVING

A *Read and listen to each problem. Choose a solution and write your reason for choosing that solution.*

Problem 1

You have just eaten in a restaurant. You couldn't stand the food, and the service was terrible. When you get your bill, you see the waiter did not write everything down, so the amount on the bill is too low.

You:

a. tell the waiter to add the things to the bill.

b. tell the cashier about the mistake when you leave.

c. don't say anything and pay the amount of the bill.

d. pay the bill and leave the extra money as a tip.

e. other: _____

Reason: _____

Problem 2

Your friend bought a new sweater. She asks what you think of it. You don't like it, but you know she can't return the sweater.

You:

a. say, "It's a beautiful sweater."

b. say, "I'm not crazy about the sweater."

c. say, "I don't like it."

d. change the subject.

e. other: _____

Reason: _____

Problem 3

You are taking a final exam. Your good friend wants to see your answers. You want to help him out, but you don't want to get into trouble.

You:

a. show him your answers and hope neither of you gets into trouble.

b. show him the answers because that's what friends are for.

c. don't show him the answers because it's wrong to cheat.

d. don't show him the answers because you don't want to get into trouble.

e. other: _____

Reason: _____

Problem 4

You were planning to buy a video at the video store. On the way to the store, you see a man on the street selling copied videos at half price.

You:

a. buy the video at the store because you aren't sure that the other video is good.

b. buy the video at the store because you think it's unfair to the people who produced the video.

c. buy the video from the man on the street.

d. buy both videos and return the video to the store when you are sure the video from the street is good.

e. other: _____

Reason: _____

B *Work in small groups. Talk about each problem in Part A and decide what your group would do.*

FROM THE NEWS

A Answer the questions.

- How can you tell if someone is lying?
- What physical changes take place when a person lies?

Now read and listen to the article.

BAD NEWS FOR LIARS

There's bad news for husbands or wives who cheat and for politicians who don't keep their promises. A new lie detector called the Handy Truster Emotion Reader exposes liars. While most other detectors, called polygraphs, measure body changes such as increased pulse rate, this one measures the sound of a voice. Its South Korean makers say it can see through eight out of ten lies.

This convenient gadget is inexpensive and small enough to fit in your pocket. You can plug it into a telephone or a cell phone, and it is more accurate than other lie detectors.

The detector shows results with an apple on a screen. If you are telling the truth, you see an uneaten apple. If you are telling a half-truth, you see some bites in the apple. If you are lying, you see the core of the apple.

B Mark the following sentences **T** *(true)* or **F** *(false)*.

_____ 1. The new lie detector measures the sound of a voice.

_____ 2. The detector is small but expensive.

_____ 3. The detector shows the results on a screen.

_____ 4. The detector is not as good as other lie detectors.

_____ 5. The detector uses a picture to show if a person is lying.

_____ 6. The detector uses words to show if a person is lying.

C Look at these sentences with a partner. Do you agree or disagree with them? Explain your opinion.

1. Good liars can pass lie detector tests.
2. Lie detectors should not be used in court cases.
3. It would be fun to use a lie detector at a party.

WORDS AND PHRASES II

A *Find and underline these words and phrases in the article on page 18.*

keep their promises	exposes	increased	small enough	accurate

B *Match the words or phrases on the left with their opposites on the right. Write the correct letter on the line.*

_____ 1. keep their promises   **a.** decreased

_____ 2. exposes   **b.** too big

_____ 3. small enough   **c.** break their promises

_____ 4. increased   **d.** not exactly correct

_____ 5. accurate   **e.** hides

ACT IT OUT

As a class, play the game "Who's the Liar?"

Use the phrases in the box to ask three students questions about their likes and dislikes. Two students answer all the questions truthfully. The third student lies some of the time. After ten minutes of questions, the class guesses who the liar is. The class also guesses which answers are not true.

ASKING ABOUT LIKES AND DISLIKES	EXPRESSING LIKES AND DISLIKES
What is your favorite *time of day*?	I love . . .
What *vegetable* do you like?	I really like . . .
What *sports* don't you like?	I like . . .
	I don't care for . . .
	I can't stand . . .

PROVERBS

Work in small groups. Discuss what these sayings mean and give examples.

> ◆ *Honesty is the best policy.*
>
> ◆ *A liar needs a good memory.*
>
> ◆ *A half-truth is a whole lie.*

BEYOND THE CLASSROOM

Think of a story from your culture about a great leader who was very honest, or a folktale about a person who was dishonest. Tell your story to the class.

EXAMPLE

Abraham Lincoln was the sixteenth president of the United States. He was one of the greatest presidents of the United States.

Lincoln was born in a log cabin in Kentucky in 1809. As he grew up, he loved to read and preferred learning to working in the fields. This led to difficulties between him and his father, and at age twenty-one he moved away.

In his twenties he moved to Illinois. There he had several jobs. He did surveying, worked as a postmaster, and had a store. Even as a young man, Lincoln showed a lot of character and honesty. Once he walked many miles just to return some change to a customer. People in that area were so impressed with his honesty that they gave him the nickname "Honest Abe." The nickname stuck with him. Lincoln is one of the few politicians with the word "honest" linked to his name.

Answers to Pronunciation B, page 13:

2. worked /t/   5. wanted /ɪd/

3. tried /d/   6. blurted /ɪd/

4. checked /t/

Love and Marriage

THINK ABOUT THE TOPIC

Where do most people meet romantic partners these days? What is one advantage and one disadvantage of each way of meeting?

- **a.** at school or work
- **b.** at dance clubs
- **c.** through matchmakers (people who introduce others for the purpose of marriage)
- **d.** through blind dates (dates arranged for people who have never met before)
- **e.** through Internet dating services
- **f.** other: _____

TALK ABOUT YOUR EXPERIENCE

A *What kind of person makes a good husband or wife? Complete the questionnaire. Write the number next to each item. Then compare your answers with a partner.*

QUESTIONNAIRE

1 = very important   2 = important   3 = not very important   4 = not important

_____ **a.** a person who can save money

_____ **b.** a person who can make enough money for a family to live well

_____ **c.** a person who can cook well

_____ **d.** a person my parents like

_____ **e.** a person who likes my parents

_____ **f.** a romantic person

_____ **g.** an honest person

_____ **h.** a hardworking person

_____ **i.** a person who stays with me when things are bad

_____ **j.** a person who laughs at the same things I do

_____ **k.** a person who loves children

_____ **l.** an attractive person

_____ **m.** a spiritual person

B *Discuss with the class.*

1. Which items are very important for the women in your class? for the men?

Women	*Men*
_____	_____
_____	_____
_____	_____

2. Does the class agree on any item?

3. Are more items "very important" for the women or the men? Why?

4. Imagine your parents are completing this questionnaire. In your opinion, would they give the same answers as you?

5. Can you think of items to add to the questionnaire?

6. Do you think people from different cultures look for different qualities?

7. As a result of your discussion, did you learn anything new about your classmates? about yourself?

LISTENING

A *Answer the questions before you listen.*

- Have you ever had a blind date or have you ever arranged a blind date for others? Did it work out?

B *Listen to the conversation. Then circle the best answer to complete the sentences.*

1. At the start of the conversation, Shira and Tom are outside a _____.
   a. park
   b. restaurant
   c. school

2. Shira and Tom _____.
   a. have met before
   b. meet by chance
   c. meet for the first time

3. Both Shira and Tom _____.
   a. are annoyed by the twins
   b. have headaches
   c. like fish

C *Work in groups. Read about the problem. Make suggestions for Shira and Tom. Then tell the class the results of your discussion.*

Shira and Tom continue to see each other. They fall in love. After ten months, they begin discussing marriage. It turns out that Shira wants a lot of children and Tom doesn't want any.

PRONUNCIATION

When a word ends with a /d/ or /t/ sound, and the following word begins with a /y/ sound, they form the new sound /tʃ/ or /dʒ/.

A *Listen to these sentences.*

- Would you like chicken or fish?
- Don't you want to come?

B *Listen as the speaker asks the questions. Pay attention to the combining sounds. Draw a link between the sounds. The first one is done for you. Check your answers on page 31.*

1. Would you like to go inside?

2. What would you like to have, salmon or sea bass?

3. Could you please bring the check?

4. Can't you understand me?

5. Won't you be late?

C *Work with a partner. Match the statements on the left with the appropriate responses on the right.*

_____ 1. Would you like to go inside?

_____ 2. What would you like to have, salmon or sea bass?

_____ 3. Could you please bring the check?

_____ 4. Can't you understand me?

_____ 5. Won't you be late?

a. No, I have plenty of time.

b. No, I'm sorry. Try speaking more slowly.

c. Yes. It looks wonderful here.

d. I'll try the salmon.

e. Certainly. I'll be back in a minute.

Listen and check your work. Then read the questions out loud. Your partner responds.

PROBLEM SOLVING

🎧 **A** *Read and listen to each problem. Choose a solution and write your reason for choosing that solution.*

Problem 1

Your friend is thinking about getting married. In your eyes, he and his girlfriend are like night and day. He gets up early. She likes to burn the midnight oil. He's ambitious; she's very laid back. He's a good cook; she can't cook at all. He hates sports; she's very athletic. He's always cheerful; she rarely smiles.

You:

a. advise your friend not to marry her.

b. wish him luck.

c. think "opposites attract."

d. other: _____

Reason: _____

Problem 2

Your nephew has introduced you to his fiancée. She's twice his age.

You:

a. advise him not to marry her because she's too old for him.

b. wish him luck; it's his life after all.

c. talk to him about the potential problems of a big age difference.

d. other: _____

Reason: _____

Problem 3

A beautiful young woman married a rich old man. It was his second marriage. Two years later at the age of 85, the man died. The woman was 26. He left this woman 5 million dollars in his will. His children are fighting the will. Who should get the man's money?

a. His wife should get the money.

b. A judge should decide.

c. The children and the wife should split the money in half.

d. other: _____

Reason: _____

(continued on next page)

Love and Marriage | 25

Problem 4

Your friend has been dating a woman for six months and he's crazy about her. They see eye to eye on almost everything. There's only one problem. She's a tightwad. She has a good job but won't buy anything unless it's on sale. Your friend is thinking about asking her to marry him. He asks your opinion. He wants to know if he's making a mistake.

You tell him:

a. she will probably make a wonderful wife.

b. it could become a problem. You suggest he wait a while and see how he feels in a few months.

c. she will never feel free to enjoy things that cost money. He will be very unhappy.

d. other: _____

Reason: _____

B *Work in small groups. Talk about each problem in Part A and decide what your group would do.*

WORDS AND PHRASES I

A *Find and underline these phrases in the Problem Solving section.*

a. like night and day	e. to be crazy about
b. to burn the midnight oil	f. to see eye to eye
c. to be laid back	g. a tightwad
d. a fiancée	

B *Write the letter of the phrase from the box in Part A next to its meaning.*

_g_ **1.** a person who hates to spend money

____ **2.** very different

____ **3.** to stay up late

____ **4.** a woman who a man is going to marry

____ **5.** to like someone or something very much

____ **6.** to be relaxed

____ **7.** to agree

FROM THE NEWS

A *Answer the questions.*

1. How important is it for your friends to like the same things you do?
2. Have you ever recommended a book to a boyfriend or girlfriend? What happened?

Now read and listen to the article.

BOOKS TO TEST TRUE LOVE

You can use a book in many ways. *New York Times* reporter Arnold Martin discovered that many women use books to measure love.

One woman told him that while dating one man, another man asked her out. She gave each man a book to read. She said, "I wanted to see if they cared enough about me to at least read a book I liked." Neither man read the book so she broke it off with both of them.

An informal survey showed that there were two books that many women chose as their test for true love. One was *Anna Karenina* by Leo Tolstoy and the other was *The Sun Also Rises* by Ernest Hemingway. The Tolstoy story is about a woman's faith in true love. The Hemingway book is a novel of drinking, fighting, wandering, and loving.

Sometimes it's not enough to just read a book. One man read *Anna Karenina*, but he identified with the wrong character.

He identified with a weak man, one without strong feelings. This certainly didn't help him win the love and admiration of the woman he wanted. According to writer Melissa Bank,". . . you are totally separated from someone when they don't get a book, or they love a book you thought was terrible."

An editorial director said, "You get tremendous insight into the character of people and their emotions from the books they like."

Of course there is no accounting for taste. For one woman, anyone who liked *The Bridges of Madison County* was off her list because the book was so sentimental. For another woman the book was the best test of a man's feelings for the very same reason.

B *Circle the letter of the correct answer.*

1. What was the main idea of the article?
   a. Women can learn about a man from the books he likes.
   b. The characters in a novel are truer than life.
   c. Men should read novels.

2. What does *identify with* mean in the phrase, "he identified with the wrong character"?
   a. didn't like
   b. caught
   c. felt the same way as

3. What does *insight* mean in the phrase, "you get tremendous insight into the character of people"?
   a. help
   b. understanding
   c. love

4. What does *get* mean in the phrase, "they don't get a book"?
   a. They don't understand it.
   b. They don't enjoy it.
   c. They don't have it.

C *Discuss in small groups.*

1. Do you agree with the quote, ". . . you are totally separated from someone when they don't get a book, or they love a book you thought was terrible"?
2. Do you think that women and men have different ideas about love?

ACT IT OUT

Act out the situation on the next page with a partner. Remember to use the language from the box.

ASKING ABOUT PREFERENCES	EXPRESSING PREFERENCES
Do you like *movies* or *plays*?	I prefer *movies.*
Would you rather go to a *museum* or a *sports event*?	I'd rather *see a play* than *an opera.*
	My favorite *kind of movie* is a *comedy.*

Situation

A dating service employee (**A**) interviews a new client (**B**).

A: You work at a dating service. Interview a new client. Ask about the client's likes and dislikes.

B: You are joining a dating service. Answer the interviewer's questions.

> EXAMPLE
>
> *A: Hi, I'm Dan Evans.*
>
> *B: I'm Derek Mark.*
>
> *A: It's good to meet you. Derek, I'd like to ask you a few questions so we can find you the perfect match.*
>
> *B: That would be great.*
>
> *A: First of all, on a first date would you prefer to go to a restaurant or a movie?*
>
> *B: I'd prefer. . .*

PROVERBS

Work in small groups. Discuss what these sayings mean and give examples.

> ◆ *Keep your eyes open before marriage, half shut afterwards.*
> —American proverb
>
> ◆ *Love is like a baby—it needs to be treated tenderly.*
> —African proverb
>
> ◆ *Love and eggs are best when they are fresh.*
> —Russian proverb

WORDS AND PHRASES II

A *The following words can be used to describe a traditional wedding in the United States. Look up new words in a dictionary. Then label the picture.*

bride	best man	music
groom	ushers	flower girl
clergyperson	bridesmaids	maid/matron of honor
flowers	photographer	

B *Work with a partner. Describe the picture on page 30 to each other. Use the words from the box in Part A.*

BEYOND THE CLASSROOM

Find out about wedding customs in two different places. Answer the following questions. Report your findings to the class.

- What do people wear?
- How long is the wedding?
- What do people eat?
- What kinds of gifts are given?

> **EXAMPLE**
>
> At a Chinese wedding banquet, eight dishes are usually served, not including dessert. In Chinese, the word for eight sounds like the word for good luck. At a traditional wedding in the United States, the bride wears "something old, something new, something borrowed, something blue."

Answers to Pronunciation B, page 24:

2. would you   4. Can't you

3. Could you   5. Won't you

The Golden Years

THINK ABOUT THE TOPIC

What are the advantages and disadvantages for older people in these situations?

- moving to a retirement community with other older people
- living in their own home apart from their children
- moving in with their children and grandchildren

TALK ABOUT YOUR EXPERIENCE

A *Answer the questions. Then ask a classmate.*

	You	Your Classmate
1. At what age do men usually retire in your country?		
2. At what age do women usually retire in your country?		
3. Do most older people you know live with their children?		
4. Have you ever lived with a grandparent? If yes, who did you live with? Were there any problems between different generations? If so, what were they?		

B *Discuss with the class.*

1. Who are some of the older people in your life now or in the past? What did they teach you?

2. What are the biggest problems for older people in your community?

LISTENING

A *Answer the questions before you listen.*

- Have you read about people who are 100 or older?
- Why do you think some people live so long?

	The Super Survivors	Sam Harlow
eat "unhealthy" food		
never very fat		
rarely smoke		
play golf		
walk		
swim		
do crossword puzzles		
watch TV		
religious		
deal well with stress		

C *Discuss in groups.*

1. Who's the oldest person you know?
2. How does this person compare to the people in the study?
3. Do you know any secrets for living a long and healthy life? What are they?

PRONUNCIATION

All words can be divided into syllables or parts. In English, one syllable gets the most stress. In the stressed syllable, the vowel is louder, longer, and a little higher. When the wrong syllable is stressed, the word is hard for people to understand.

⌒ **A** *Listen to these words.*

	Syllables
eat	1
heal · thy	2
un · **heal** · thy	3
cel · e · brat · ed	4

1. un(heal)thy foods
2. ladies and gentlemen
3. super survivors
4. probably good advice
5. similar habits
6. we're delighted
7. it's been wonderful
8. physically active

PROBLEM SOLVING

🎧 **A** *Read and listen to each problem. Choose a solution and write your reason for choosing that solution.*

Problem 1

You have a seat on a bus. An older woman gets on the bus. There are no empty seats.

You:

a. give up your seat.

b. ask a child to give up his or her seat.

c. keep your seat and look the other way.

d. other: _____

Reason: _____

Problem 2

You get on the bus at the same time as a frail older man. All the seats on the bus are taken. Nobody gives the man a seat.

You:

a. ask a young person to give the old man a seat.

b. use gestures to suggest that someone give the man a seat.

c. don't do anything since you don't have a seat to give him.

d. other: _____

Reason: _____

(continued on next page)

You live in a town of 10,000 people. Very few people are over sixty-five. The city planners want to build 2,000 apartments for older citizens. You want your tax money to go for schools and parks. Some say the older people will vote against spending money on such things.

You vote:

a. for these apartments.

b. against these apartments.

c. for some apartments, but not so many.

d. other: _____

Reason: _____

Your boss said you can hire a part-time assistant. Two people have applied for the job. One is a college student with no work experience. The other is a retired person with many years of experience. They are both excellent typists, have excellent computer skills, and sound good on the telephone. Both did well on the interview.

You:

a. hire the younger person. That person is more flexible.

b. hire the younger person. That person is cheaper.

c. hire the older person. That person has more experience.

d. other: _____

Reason: _____

B *Work in small groups. Talk about each problem in Part A and decide what your group would do.*

FROM THE NEWS

A *Answer the questions.*

Do you agree with this statement? Why or why not?

• Forcing older people to retire helps younger people get better jobs.

Now read and listen to the article.

FORCED RETIREMENT IN CANADA IS A DINOSAUR

Canada has a law that forces people to retire at the age of sixty-five. Keith Norton is the Human Rights Commissioner in Ontario, Canada. He believes this law is bad for Canadians. He thinks people should be allowed to work beyond sixty-five if they want to. In some countries such as the United States and New Zealand, it is against the law to force people to retire because of their age.

Commissioner Norton points out that there are economic and social reasons to end forced retirement. In Canada, the percentage of older people is rapidly growing. In 1960, Canadians over sixty-five were 7.6 percent of the population. Today they are over 12 percent of the population. By 2030, they will be over 20 percent of the population. This could mean fewer people will provide for the needs of the country. And this will hurt the economy.

A study by the Organization for Economic Cooperation and Development (OECD) pointed out that many men in countries like Canada are spending at least half of their lives not working. This is not good for a society. Most healthy people feel better when they are working. "Individuals should be as free as possible to decide when they retire," the OECD study says. If someone is unhealthy or if someone has enough money to support himself or herself, a person may wish to give up work. But public programs should not encourage early retirement. And employers should not force retirement.

One argument for early retirement programs is that they allow companies to hire more younger workers. But the OECD study says that there is no evidence that this is what happens in most cases.

So according to Commissioner Norton, it is time for Canada to join the United States and New Zealand and end forced retirement.

B *Circle the letter of the correct answer according to the article.*

1. What does the title of the article mean?
   a. Forcing people to retire is an old-fashioned idea.
   b. When people retire, they become like dinosaurs.
   c. Forced retirement is good for Canada.

(continued on next page)

2. What is one economic reason to end forced retirement?
   a. Too many people will be working in the future.
   b. Too few people will be working in the future.
   c. People who retire spend a lot of money.

3. What is one social reason to end forced retirement?
   a. Work is good for people's mental health.
   b. You can have parties when you don't work.
   c. Younger people need jobs.

C *Discuss with the class.*

1. Is there discrimination against older people in your area? In what ways?
2. How should society help older people?
3. Why should society help older people?

WORDS AND PHRASES

A *Find and underline these phrases in the news article on page 37.*

| to hire | to retire | to support himself or herself | to give up |

B *Match the words or phrases on the left with their opposites on the right. Write the letter on the line.*

_____ 1. to hire   **a.** to be financially dependent

_____ 2. to retire from work   **b.** to keep working

_____ 3. to support oneself   **c.** to fire

_____ 4. to give up work   **d.** to start work

C *Complete the sentences with your own ideas. Answer the questions in parentheses.*

1. _____My friend_____ hired someone to __paint his house__ .
   (who?)   (what?)

2. _____ retired _____.
   (who?)   (when?)

3. In _____ they discriminated against _____.
   (where?)   (whom?)

4. _____ supported _____.
   (who?)   (whom?)

5. When he _____, he gave up _____.
   (what?)   (what?)

ACT IT OUT

Act out the situation with a partner. Remember to use the language from the box.

ASKING FOR SUGGESTIONS	GIVING ADVICE/EXPLAINING CONSEQUENCES
What do you think he/she should do? What do you suggest? What would you do?	I think he should . . . I don't think she should . . . I think he ought to . . . If she . . . , she will be able to . . . If he . . . , he won't be able to . . . If I were her, I would . . .

Situation

You and your friend are discussing another friend's situation. The other friend has found an apartment to share with a roommate. The apartment is perfect, but the roommate is over sixty years old. Your friend is twenty.

Discuss the advantages and disadvantages of your friend's situation.

PROVERBS

Work in small groups. Discuss what these sayings mean and give examples.

> ◆ *One mother can take care of six children, but six children cannot take care of one mother.*
>
> ◆ *It is not how old you are, but how you are old.*
>
> ◆ *Age is something that doesn't matter, unless you are a cheese.*
>
> ◆ *Cherish youth, but trust old age.*

BEYOND THE CLASSROOM

Traditional cultures teach children to respect and care for older people. Find or make up a folktale about an older person. Tell it to the class.

EXAMPLE

Joe's eighty-year-old father came to visit. The older man spent the afternoon playing with his young grandson Billy. Before leaving, the older man said to his son Joe, "I'm sorry to bother you, but winter is coming. My house is cold. Winter is long."

Joe looked annoyed and said, "Father, you know I'd like to help you, but I have so many expenses. Maybe next year."

The older man quickly answered, "Oh, I understand."

As he was about to leave, Joe turned to Billy and said, "Billy, run upstairs. Bring down that old winter coat for Grandpa."

Billy ran upstairs and came down with the coat. He looked at his father and grandfather and tore the coat in two. Joe shouted, "Billy! Why did you tear that coat in two?"

The child looked at his father and quietly said, "I'm saving the other half for you."

Answers to Pronunciation B, page 35:

2. (gen)tlemen   4. (pro)bably   6. de(li)ghted   8. (ac)tive

3. sur(vi)vors   5. (si)milar   7. (won)derful

Borrowing and Lending

THINK ABOUT THE TOPIC

1. Who is lending something and who is borrowing something in each picture?
2. How do the father, the sister, and the friend feel about lending something?
3. What are the advantages and disadvantages of borrowing or lending things?

TALK ABOUT YOUR EXPERIENCE

A *Read all the statements. Check (✓) the statements you agree with. Then ask a classmate.*

	You	Your Classmate
1. I try not to borrow or lend money. If I have to borrow money, I go to a bank. I don't like to ask friends or relatives for money.		
2. I don't like to borrow or lend money. If I really need money, I reluctantly ask my family or close friends.		
3. I don't mind lending money to friends and relatives who need it. If I need money, I don't mind asking my friends or relatives.		
4. I don't mind lending money to friends or relatives, but I hate to borrow it from anyone.		

B *Discuss with the class.*

1. Do you and your classmate have the same attitude about borrowing and lending money? Which statement got the most checks in your class?

2. Do you think that borrowing or lending money among friends and relatives is more common in some cultures than in others? Where else do people you know go to borrow money?

3. Have you ever borrowed a friend's clothes? Car? Cell phone? CDs? Jewelry? Apartment? Did anything unexpected happen? Explain.

LISTENING

A *Answer the question before you listen.*

- Would you let friends with children stay in your home while you were away?

B *Listen to the conversation between a husband and wife. Check (✓) all true statements.*

_____ **1.** Mike and Melissa recently moved to the West Coast.

_____ **2.** Melissa doesn't work.

_____ **3.** The couple in the conversation has known Mike and Melissa for a long time.

_____ **4.** Mike and Melissa want to go to Mexico.

_____ **5.** Melissa doesn't like her mother-in-law.

_____ **6.** Mike doesn't get along with his mother-in-law.

_____ **7.** Mike and Melissa's children are not very disciplined.

_____ **8.** The man in the conversation doesn't want Mike and Melissa to stay in his apartment.

_____ **9.** At the end of the conversation, the woman agrees with the man.

PRONUNCIATION

When we speak, we often use a contraction of will and the word that comes before it.

A *Listen and repeat these sentences.*

1. I'll be back.
2. She'll help.
3. You'll be sorry.
4. It'll cost a lot.
5. He'll be there.
6. We'll see them soon.
7. They'll break something.
8. The kids'll help.
9. What'll you say?

B *Go back and listen to the conversation in Listening B again. Complete the sentences. Use a contraction of* will *where necessary. Check your answers on page 49.*

1. That's when _____ in Mexico.
2. The _____ something or _____ door unlocked or do some other _____.
3. _____ our friendship for sure.
4. _____ tell them?
5. _____ of something to say.

C *Take turns reading each sentence to a partner.*

WORDS AND PHRASES I

A *Complete the story with the correct form of the words or phrases from the box.*

lend	credit history	borrow	charge (someone) interest
IOU*	earn interest	pay back	rate of interest

*IOU = I owe you

When Carmen and her husband moved to a new country, they needed money to open a business. The bank refused to _____ them
₁ money because they didn't have a _____.
₂

Carmen went to her brother and asked to _____ the money.
₃ He agreed to lend her the money, but said, "My money is in the bank, where it's _____. I'll lend you the money if you pay me the same
₄ _____ as the bank."
₅

Carmen took the money and gave her brother an _____. In
₆ five years, she _____ the money and the interest. She never told
₇ her brother how she felt, but she could not forget that he had _____
₈ _____.

B *Ask a partner.*

1. In your opinion, was the brother right?
2. How would you have acted as the brother? As the sister?

PROBLEM SOLVING

 A *Read and listen to each problem. Choose a solution and write your reason for choosing that solution.*

Problem 1

A classmate asks to borrow $30. You don't know her very well.

You:

a. lend her the money and hope to get it back.

b. lend her the money but ask for an IOU.

c. make an excuse.

d. other: _____

Reason: _____

Problem 2

A good friend owes you $100. He promised to pay you back two months ago. You reminded him about it twice in the past three weeks.

Now you:

a. forget about the money. Your friendship is worth more than $100.

b. speak to him again.

c. ask your lawyer to send him a letter.

d. other: _____

Reason: _____

Problem 3

You borrowed your friend's cell phone. You dropped it and the cover broke. The phone still works, but you can't reattach the cover. Your friend said, "Don't worry about it," but you feel bad. However, you don't have an extra $150 to replace the phone.

You:

a. forget about it.

b. keep your friend's phone and get him a new one.

c. buy him a leather cell phone case.

d. other: _____

Reason: _____

Problem 4

You got married a few months ago. You and your spouse both work far from your home. You each take two buses and a train to get to work. Your in-laws rarely use their car. They want to lend it to you. Your spouse wants to use it, but you don't.

You:

a. borrow their car to please your spouse.

b. tell your spouse to use the car, but you continue to take the buses and train.

c. don't borrow their car. Everyone will feel terrible if something happens to it.

d. other: _____

Reason: _____

B *Work in small groups. Talk about each problem in Part A and decide what your group would do.*

FROM THE NEWS

A *Answer the questions.*

- Have you ever lent a large amount of money to a relative? If so, what happened?

Now read and listen to the article.

BE CAREFUL WHEN LENDING TO RELATIVES

It's not unusual to want to help family members by lending money, especially when a bank won't. It's also not unusual for that IOU to change the relationship, and not necessarily for the better, experts say. "Each may have expectations about how one is going to handle the debt," says psychiatrist Carol Watkins. "The person who gets the money, in some cases, may have the feeling that because they got the money from a relative, this particular debt is a lower priority to pay back."

The other person may see it differently.

Financial advisers give this advice to people who plan to lend money to relatives.

- Go in with open eyes. If a bank won't lend your relative money, there's a reason.

- Get the loan in writing. It's easy for both sides to forget or get confused about the exact deal. It's also a way to show that the money is a loan and not a gift.

continued

- Check the tax laws of your country. In the United States, for example, the government makes lenders charge interest for loans of more than $10,000. Also, the person who gets the money has to report the income.

The bottom line on family loans is this: Don't lend any money you can't afford to lose.

B *Circle the best answer to complete the sentences according to the article.*

1. If you lend a relative money, _____.
   a. you won't get it back
   b. your relative will be grateful
   c. your relationship may change

2. The person who borrowed money may believe _____.
   a. this loan is a top priority to pay back
   b. this loan isn't as important as other debts
   c. the person who lent the money is rich

3. The expression "go in with open eyes" means _____.
   a. understand all sides of a situation
   b. look everywhere
   c. don't sleep too much

4. "The bottom line" means _____.
   a. what's really important
   b. winning is everything
   c. last is best

C *Discuss with a partner.*

1. What would be a good reason for you to borrow money from a relative?
2. Would you lend someone money for the same reason?

WORDS AND PHRASES II

Complete the sentences with words from the box. Consult a dictionary if necessary.

dependents	reference	previous address
salary	bankrupt	present address

1. Many small businesses go _____ during a recession.
2. The place where you used to live is your _____.
3. People you support are your _____.
4. The money you make from your job is your _____.
5. A friend or relative who can give a bank information about you is a _____.
6. The place where you now live is your _____.

ACT IT OUT

Act out the situation below with a partner. Use the language from the box.

MAKING FORMAL INTRODUCTIONS; STATING A BUSINESS PURPOSE	MAKING FORMAL INTRODUCTIONS; ASKING ABOUT A BUSINESS PURPOSE
Hello. I'm *Mike Miller*. I'm interested in applying for *a mortgage.* / *a car loan.*	Nice to meet you, *Mike*. Please sit down. I'm *Emily Thomas*. What can I do for you? Let me give you *an application.* / *some information.*

Situation

A: You go to a bank for a loan. Introduce yourself to the banker and tell the banker the kind of loan you're interested in. Find out the rate of interest and the time you have to pay back the loan.

B: You are the banker. Introduce yourself and find out what **A** wants. Answer **A's** questions and give **A** a loan application. Find out **A's** previous address, present address, and salary. Find out if he or she has any dependents.

PROVERBS

Read these proverbs and answer the questions that follow.

◆ *Neither a borrower nor a lender be.*
—William Shakespeare, author

◆ *A bank is a place where they lend you an umbrella in fair weather and ask for it back when it begins to rain.*
—Robert Frost, American poet

◆ *If a man empties his purse into his head, no man can take it away from him. An investment in knowledge always pays the best interest.*
—Benjamin Franklin, American statesman, philosopher, and inventor

1. Which person has a bad opinion of banks?
2. Which person believes that knowledge is your best investment?
3. Which person doesn't believe in borrowing or lending?
4. Do you have any expressions like these in your language? What are they?

BEYOND THE CLASSROOM

Go to a bank and find answers to these questions. Report your findings to the class.

1. How do I open a savings and a checking account at this bank?
2. Do savings accounts pay interest? How much? How about checking accounts?
3. Do I have to keep a minimum amount of money in the bank? What is the minimum?
4. How much do the checks cost?
5. What other fees does the bank charge?

Answers to Pronunciation B, page 44:

1. we'll be
2. kids'll break, leave the, awful thing
3. It'll end
4. What'll you
5. I'll think

Say the Right Thing

THINK ABOUT THE TOPIC

1. Which people said the wrong thing? Explain.
2. Have you ever had experiences like those of the people in the pictures? What happened?

TALK ABOUT YOUR EXPERIENCE

A *Look at the questions and decide if and when they are impolite. Check (✓) the appropriate column. Then compare your answers with a classmate's.*

	Always Impolite	Sometimes Impolite	Never Impolite
1. How old are you?			
2. How much do you weigh?			
3. How much money do you make?			
4. Why aren't you married?			
5. Why don't you have children?			
6. Who did you vote for?			
7. Are you wearing perfume?			
8. Are you (Chinese, Polish, French)?			

B *What's another question that may be impolite? Write it below.*

_____?

C *Discuss with the class.*

1. Did you and your classmate agree on which questions were impolite and which were acceptable?

2. Are there questions that are acceptable in some cultures but not polite in others? Explain.

3. What makes a question impolite?

4. Read the impolite question you wrote in Part B to the class. Explain why you feel it is impolite. What do your classmates think?

LISTENING

A *Answer the questions before you listen.*

- When you were a child or teenager, did your parents ever do something that embarrassed you? What was it?

B *Listen to the conversation. Check (✓) all true statements.*

_____ **1.** A woman goes to her son's school to find out how he is doing.

_____ **2.** The husband didn't want to go to the meeting.

_____ **3.** The teacher says Danny sings well.

_____ **4.** The teacher says Danny doesn't get along well with the other children.

_____ **5.** Danny is forgetful.

_____ **6.** Danny is a poor student.

_____ **7.** Danny's mother is too embarrassed to get her coat.

_____ **8.** Danny's mother is angry at Danny.

_____ **9.** Danny and his mother are alike.

C *Discuss in small groups.*

1. If Danny asks his mother about her meeting with his teacher, what should she tell him?

2. How old do you think Danny is? Why?

PRONUNCIATION

There are three ending sounds for third person singular verbs in the simple present tense: /s/, /z/, and /ɪz/.

A *Listen to the present tense verbs.*

/s/	/z/	/ɪz/
walks	lives	catches

B *Listen to each sentence. Underline the third person singular verbs in the simple present tense. Then write the correct sound above each verb ending that you underlined. Check your answers on page 59.*

1. Ms. Cook said he <u>/z/
reads</u> and <u>/s/
writes</u> very well.

2. She also said he gets along well with others.

3. And he never misses a note.

4. She said she wishes he wouldn't be so forgetful.

5. Not for me, but she seems to think so.

C *Practice reading the sentences with a partner.*

WORDS AND PHRASES

A *Complete the story with the words from the box.*

into	out	over	get	hide

Last summer, my wife and I took a cruise along the St. Lawrence River in Canada. We shared our meals with four other couples. While they all remembered my name, I couldn't _____ their names straight. I managed

<u>1</u>

to _____ my ignorance for a couple of days, but by the third day I asked

<u>2</u>

my wife to help me _____. We went _____ their names and

<u>3</u>   <u>4</u>

nicknames until I felt I knew them all. The next morning, I ran _____

<u>5</u>

one of the couples at the shuffleboard court. The woman called out, "Hi, Sam.

How's it going?" I replied, "Great, Joliette." She laughed and said, "Nice try, Sam.

But that's not my name. I'm Julia. Joliette was the city we visited last night."

B *Complete the sentences using the words from the box.*

| disease | face | compliments | foot | red |

1. When his mom kissed him after the game, he turned beet _____.
2. I really wanted to laugh, but I had to be serious. It was hard to keep a straight _____.
3. He always says embarrassing things. He suffers from foot-in-mouth _____.
4. When I first started my job, I said the wrong thing to my boss. We started off on the wrong _____.
5. Last night my aunt said she was surprised I could cook so well. She has a habit of giving left-handed _____.

C *Match the idioms on the left with their definitions on the right. Write the letter on the line.*

_____ **1.** start off on the wrong foot   **a.** get embarrassed

_____ **2.** keep a straight face   **b.** a comment that is positive, but a little negative too

_____ **3.** foot-in-mouth disease

_____ **4.** turn beet red   **c.** have a bad beginning

_____ **5.** a left-handed compliment   **d.** be serious when you want to laugh

    e. a habit of saying the wrong thing

PROBLEM SOLVING

A *Read and listen to each problem on the next page. Choose a solution and write your reason for choosing that solution.*

Problem 1

You have a part-time job in a store. Your boss gave you a raise last month but said, "I want to give you more money than your co-workers because you work harder. But please don't tell the others." Yesterday one of your co-workers asked, "How much money are you making? I'm getting $7 an hour. Are you getting more?"

You answer:

a. "Yes, I'm getting $8 an hour, but please don't tell anyone."

b. "I'm earning about the same as you."

c. "None of your business."

d. other: _____

Reason: _____

Problem 2

You meet a friend you haven't seen for a few months. You ask, "How's your husband?" She replies, "We got divorced two months ago."

You say:

a. "I'm really sorry to hear that."

b. "Good for you. I never liked him."

c. "Why?"

d. other: _____

Reason: _____

Problem 3

Two years ago, your favorite nephew became the director of his company in a far-away country. Upon arriving in your city on business, he invites you to dinner. When you see him, you're shocked. He looks ten years older. He has gained about thirty pounds. He smokes at least ten cigarettes during dinner.

You:

a. don't say anything about his appearance.

b. wait for him to say something about his appearance.

c. make a joke about how he has changed.

d. other: _____

Reason: _____

B *Work in small groups. Talk about each problem in Part A and decide what your group would do.*

FROM THE NEWS

A *Answer the questions.*

- Are you good at remembering people's names?
- What can you do to help yourself remember a person's name?

Now read and listen to the article.

REMEMBERING NAMES

I ran into a friend the other day but had forgotten his name. I know that he had forgotten mine, too. How do you get out of such an embarrassing situation? Here are some suggestions from readers:

Bring in a third person. Pretend you know that person. The third person will (with luck) be too polite to say that he has never met you. You say to the third person, "I'm terribly sorry, but I've forgotten your name." This person will then introduce himself. You can then introduce yourself. Your friend will now introduce himself. Now you have discovered your friend's name, and he yours, without showing your ignorance.

Barbara Plunkett,
Lincoln, England

Move to France. "Bonjour monsieur/madame" is quite acceptable if you don't know someone really well.

Charles Ward-Jackson,
London, England

The orchestra conductor Sir Thomas Beecham told this story: After conducting a concert, he vaguely recognized a woman who started a conversation with him. When she mentioned her brother, Beecham saw his chance. He asked about her brother's health and asked if he was still doing the same job. "Oh, yes," she replied, "he is very well and is still king."

Mark Hebert,
Needingworth, England

You could try the Samoan method. There, people greet one another with their own name. So Dick Collins would say in Samoa, "Hi, Dick Collins!" And Jonathan Green would answer, "Hi, Jonathan Green."

Dick Collins,
County Cork, Ireland

B *Mark the following sentences* **T** *(true), or* **F** *(false).*

_____ **1.** Barbara Plunkett thinks that you can find out a person's name without asking the person by bringing in a third person.

_____ **2.** Barbara Plunkett thinks it's OK to show your ignorance.

_____ **3.** It's very important to remember names in France.

_____ **4.** The conductor Sir Thomas Beecham wanted to hide his ignorance.

_____ **5.** The conductor Sir Thomas Beecham spoke to the sister of a king.

_____ **6.** If you meet Bill Jones in Samoa, you say, "Hi, Bill."

C *Discuss with the class.*

1. Do you think the Samoan system for greeting people is a good one?
2. Do you have any other suggestions for people who forget names?

ACT IT OUT

Act out the situation with a partner. Use the language from the box.

CONFIRMING INFORMATION	CONTRADICTING SOMEONE
Aren't you *Brad Pitt*? **OR** You're *Brad Pitt*, aren't you?	I'm afraid you're mistaken. I'm not . . .
Don't you *work in the bank*? **OR** You *work in the bank*, don't you?	You must be mistaken. I don't . . .
Weren't you *my third-grade teacher*? **OR** You were *my third grade teacher*, weren't you?	I don't think so. I wasn't . . .

Situation

A: You're sure that you know **B**. You greet **B** and discover that you've made a mistake. Continue the conversation. Get to know **B**.

B: A stranger (**A**) greets you in the street, but calls you by the wrong name. Tell **A** that he or she is mistaken. Continue the conversation. Get to know **A**.

PROVERBS

Read the proverb. Why does man need to blush?

◆ *Man is the only animal that blushes. Or needs to.*
   —Mark Twain, American writer

Can you explain the following saying?

◆ *He opens his mouth only long enough to change feet.*

BEYOND THE CLASSROOM

Misunderstandings due to cultural differences often cause red faces. More and more companies conduct business internationally and give their workers cross-cultural training so that they don't make mistakes.

A *The following are some mistakes that North American businesspeople have made in the past. Work in small groups. Try to explain what the mistakes were. See page 59 for the answers.*

- An American businessman gave a Chinese businessman a clock as a gift.

- The Chevrolet car manufacturer had trouble selling the Chevrolet Nova in Puerto Rico.

- An American businessman received the business card of a customer in Japan. He smiled, quickly put the card in his pocket, and continued talking.

- An American businessman in Brazil indicated that something was "OK" by forming a circle with his thumb and index finger.

B *Tell the class some cultural differences you know about. For example, talk about body language, holidays or events, language differences, greetings, and eating habits that are different in your region. Tell why businesspeople need to know such things.*

EXAMPLE

> *Don't expect to do business on the day of or the day after a World Cup final in Brazil when Brazil is a finalist.*

Answers to Pronunciation B, page 53:

2. gets /s/   4. wishes /ɪz/

3. misses /ɪz/   5. seems /z/

Answers to Beyond the Classroom A, page 58:

- In Chinese, the word for *clock* sounds like the word for *death*.
- In Spanish, *nova* sounds like the words for *doesn't go*.
- In Japan, a business card is regarded as one's face. You shouldn't write on it or put it in your back pocket. Hold it carefully, read it, and put it in a business card wallet.
- Forming a circle with the thumb and index finger is an impolite gesture in Brazil.

Say the Right Thing | 59

Dress for Success

A

B

C

THINK ABOUT THE TOPIC

1. Why are the people in the pictures upset?
2. Have you ever felt like any of the people in the pictures? What happened?

TALK ABOUT YOUR EXPERIENCE

A *What's important for you when you shop for clothes? Rank the items from 1–6. (1 is the most important).*

_____ color

_____ style

_____ comfort

_____ price

_____ how it looks on you

_____ the (designer's) label

Compare your ranking with a classmate's.

B *Discuss with the class.*

1. Did you and your classmates rank the items the same way?

2. Would you ever wear the following clothes? If so, where?
   a. torn clothes
   b. worn clothes
   c. dirty clothes
   d. very modern clothes
   e. very tight clothes
   f. very conservative clothes

3. In what ways can an inappropriate outfit hurt you?

LISTENING

A *Answer the questions before you listen.*

1. What styles are popular today?

2. Do the outfits in the pictures on page 62 fit today's fashion? Why or why not?

🎧 **B** *Listen and write each model's name next to her picture. Then listen again and complete the sentences with the words from the box.*

Names:

Kate Harlow	Amy Khalid
Jennifer Ledesma	Sophia Sugar

pearl	khaki	hair	capri	leather	confidence
date	red	knee	school	quality	

Model's name _____

1. The jacket is made of _____. You could wear this outfit for a casual _____ or a night of dancing.

Model's name _____

2. The color of the pants suit is _____. The speaker thinks the pants suit looks good on the model because of her _____.

Model's name _____

3. The skirt is _____ length.
4. The model is wearing a _____ necklace and earrings. The speaker thinks this outfit shouts _____ and _____.

Model's name _____

5. The color of the pants is _____. They are called _____ pants.
6. The speaker thinks this outfit is good for _____ or play.

C *Discuss with the class.*

- Do you agree with the woman who thinks there's a bad side to fashion shows? Explain.

PRONUNCIATION

Stressing the correct syllable is important for understanding. Sometimes numbers, like fourteen and forty, sound similar. To help comprehension, you can stress the second syllable in fourteen and the first in forty.

A *Listen to the example.*

Was that four**teen** (14) or **for**ty (40)?

B *Listen to these questions. Underline the part of the number word that is stressed. Check your answers on page 69.*

1. Was that thir<u>teen</u>   or   <u>thir</u>ty?
2. Was that fifteen   or   fifty?
3. Was that seventeen   or   seventy?
4. Was that eighteenth   or   eightieth?
5. Was that nineteenth   or   ninetieth?

C *Listen and write the missing numbers in the following sentences. Check your answers on page 69.*

1. This is our _____ fashion show.
2. He's _____ years old, but he acts like he's _____.
3. Whether you're _____ or _____, you'll love this show.

D Work with a partner. Take turns saying the numbers in the box. Your partner will point to the number he or she hears.

90	30	13	14	18
40	15	50	60	17
19	16	60	70	80

PROBLEM SOLVING

A Read and listen to each problem. Choose a solution and write your reason for choosing that solution.

Problem 1

You are late for a school or a job interview. You notice a button is missing on your suit.

You:

a. sew on the button, though it will make you arrive even later.

b. change clothes even though your other suit is a little tight on you.

c. go without the button.

d. put a funny pin where the button was.

e. other: _____

Reason: _____

Problem 2

You are at a party. Someone is wearing exactly the same outfit as you.

You:

a. avoid that person.

b. leave the party immediately.

c. say to that person, "You have good taste. I like your outfit."

d. ask that person, "Where did you buy your outfit? How much did you pay?"

e. other: _____

Reason: _____

B *Work in small groups. Talk about each problem in Part A and decide what your group would do.*

FROM THE NEWS

A *Answer the questions.*

1. What is an image?
2. What is your image of yourself?
3. Do you think that you see yourself as others see you?

Now read and listen to the article.

YOUR IMAGE AT WORK

Forget experience—image is the most valuable currency in the modern workplace. Image consultant Mary Spillane points out the different factors that could be standing between you and success.

She has a business which she calls "self-branding." This means putting yourself together as an attractive package that you can market effectively. According to Spillane, career success in the twenty-first century no longer depends on certificates or even on experience.

Companies send their top executives to Spillane. Her job is to bring out the best in them. Helping people, she says, depends more on their age than on their field.

According to Spillane, today's "twenty-somethings" are a particularly difficult group. A few pointers for them: When dining, stay in your seat. Have interesting ideas for conversation that don't revolve around work, and avoid boring topics like where everyone is going on vacation this year.

To people in their thirties who are climbing the corporate ladder,

(continued on next page)

Spillane says, "Look as though you could be running things." Also, if you're moving up, you may have enemies. Learn to look as if you love someone you don't like or even can't stand. The secret lies in "pulling" them in with your eyes.

If you're over forty, you're near the top of your career. The main worry is the young things snapping at your heels. "You need to be modern without feeling an idiot," says Spillane. "Keep an eye on how music is changing and see some current films, so you aren't asking 'Joaquin who?' Don't load your hair with lacquer. Stiff hair means a stiff mind-set," says Spillane. And stay up-to-date: Get a palmtop, and don't fax things—e-mail them.

B *Circle the best answer to complete the sentences according to the article.*

1. The main idea of the article is that _____.
   a. your experience is more important than your college degree
   b. you must always pretend to love people, even if you hate them
   c. how you look and behave can help you succeed or fail at your job

2. Helping people, according to Spillane, depends mostly on their _____.
   a. profession
   b. age
   c. sex

3. The phrase "an attractive package that you can market effectively" means _____.
   a. a beautiful box
   b. a look that will help you sell yourself
   c. a store that sells a lot of things

4. The phrase to "look as though you could be running things" means to _____.
   a. look like an athlete
   b. do things quickly
   c. look like a leader

WORDS AND PHRASES

A *Label the clothes or parts of the clothes on the model. Use the words from the box.*

button	sleeves	collar	pants	cuff	cap

1. _____

2. _____

3. _____

4. _____

5. _____

6. _____

B *Now complete the idioms using words from the box.*

1. Roll up your _____ and get to work. We need your help.

2. He didn't have time to prepare in advance. Everything he said was off the _____.

3. My aunt is never late. She always arrives right on the _____.

4. You should be proud of yourself. That's a real feather in your _____.

5. His mom makes all the decisions. It's easy to see who wears the _____ in that family.

6. My boss got a little hot under the _____ when he found out everyone had left early last Friday.

C *Match the idioms on the left with their definitions on the right. Write the correct letter on the line.*

____ 1. roll up your sleeves   **a.** do or say something exactly

____ 2. off the cuff   **b.** angry about something

____ 3. right on the button   **c.** get ready to work hard

____ 4. feather in your cap   **d.** makes decisions in the family

____ 5. wears the pants   **e.** without advance preparation

____ 6. hot under the collar   **f.** an achievement you are proud of

ACT IT OUT

A *With a partner, make two lists of clothing. List singular items in one list and plural items in the other list.*

Singular	Plural
a hat	pants
_____	_____
_____	_____
_____	_____
_____	_____

B *Act out the situation with a partner. Use the language from the box.*

MAKING A COMPLAINT	RESOLVING A COMPLAINT

hat   *big.*
This *jacket* is much too *small.*
   shirt   *dark.*
 	
   pants   *baggy.*
These *jeans* are way too *tight.*
   shoes   *small.*
 	
This *jacket* isn't *long* enough.
These *gloves* aren't *warm* enough.
	I see what you mean.
	
	I'm sorry. We can't return your money,
	   but we can give you credit.
	
	I'm sorry. Do you want to exchange it/them?

Situation

A: You are a customer in a department store. You want to return an item of clothing.

B: You are a salesperson helping the customer.

> EXAMPLE
>
> A: *Excuse me. I bought these gloves last week and they're much too big for me.*
>
> B: *I see what you mean. Do you have your receipt?*
>
> A: *No, but all the labels are on the gloves.*
>
> B: *Do you want to exchange them?*

PROVERBS

Work in small groups. Discuss what these sayings mean and give examples.

> ◆ *You can't judge a book by its cover.*
>
> —American proverb
>
> ◆ *Clothes are wings.*
>
> —Korean proverb
>
> ◆ *When you meet a person, judge her by her clothes. But when you leave a person, judge her by her heart.*
>
> —Russian proverb

BEYOND THE CLASSROOM

1. Bring a picture of an unusual outfit to class. It can be from a magazine, from the Internet, or a photograph. Display your picture in the classroom. Your teacher will number all the pictures.

2. Take turns with your classmates. Tell about one of the pictures, but not the one you brought in. Describe the outfit in the picture. Give details about color and clothing type.

3. Give your opinion about the outfit in the picture. Begin by completing the following sentences.
   - This outfit would look good on a _____ (*young/middle-aged/older*) person.
   - It would be appropriate for _____ (*a job interview/a day at school/a party*). I _____ (*would/wouldn't*) wear this outfit because _____.
   - I _____ (*like/don't like*) the outfit because _____.

4. Your classmates guess the picture you are describing.

Answers to Pronunciation B, page 63:	Answers to Pronunciation C, page 63:
2. <u>fif</u>teen / <u>fif</u>ty	1. 13th
3. seven<u>teen</u> / <u>seven</u>ty	2. 40, 14
4. eigh<u>teenth</u> / <u>eigh</u>tieth	3. 16, 60
5. nine<u>teen</u> / <u>nine</u>tieth	

Medical Questions

THINK ABOUT THE TOPIC

A *Read the conversation. Fill in the name of a disease. Write the doctor's response to Mrs. Evans.*

B *Discuss the following questions with the class.*

1. *Doctor-patient confidentiality* is the promise that a doctor will not tell anyone about a patient's health. Why is this important?

2. Are there times when this confidentiality should be broken? When?

TALK ABOUT YOUR EXPERIENCE

A *Answer the questions. Then ask a classmate.*

	You	Your Classmate
1. Do you have a family doctor?		
2. How long have you gone to your doctor?		
3. About how often do you have a medical checkup?		
4. Do you like your doctor? Is your doctor open and easy to talk to? Is he or she easy to reach?		
5. Have you ever considered becoming a doctor? Why or why not?		
6. When you are sick, do you ask anyone other than your doctor for advice? Who?		
7. Have you used types of medicine or treatment other than Western ones? What types? Chinese herbal? Acupuncture? Massage?		

B *Answer the questions in the chart. Then work in small groups. Discuss your answers.*

Do you think doctors should:

	Yes	No	It depends
a. tell patients the truth about their illnesses?			
b. tell patients the side effects of medication?			
c. tell patients all the risks of medical procedures?			
d. never tell anyone what patients tell them?			

C *Discuss with the class.*

When is it OK for doctors to:

- break confidentiality?
- hide the truth about a patient's illness from the patient?
- not tell a patient about possible side effects of medications?
- not tell a patient all the possible dangers of a medical procedure?

LISTENING

A *Answer the questions before you listen.*

1. Genes determine the color of your hair and your eyes, your height, and even your personality. Today scientists are learning how to alter genes. What are the benefits of altering genes?

2. What are the dangers of altering genes?

B *Listen to the interview. Then listen again and check (✓) all true statements. More than one statement may be true.*

1. Jonas Laboratories:
   _____ **a.** has been doing research with genes for the past six years.
   _____ **b.** has produced new drugs as a result of their research.
   _____ **c.** hopes to produce new drugs as a result of their research.
   _____ **d.** is part of Jonas Pharmaceuticals.

2. Protesters at Jonas Laboratories:
   _____ **a.** believe that genes should not be altered.
   _____ **b.** are against all research.
   _____ **c.** think that only rich people will be able to alter their genes.
   _____ **d.** are against rich people.

C *Discuss with the class.*

1. Should Jonas Laboratories close or remain open? Why?
2. Should biotechnology be closely watched? Do you agree or disagee with Joe Chambers?

PRONUNCIATION

Produce, record, permit, and *conflict* can be nouns or verbs. When these words are nouns, the stress is on the first syllable. When they are verbs, the stress is on the second syllable.

A **Produce, record, permit** and **conflict** *are nouns in these sentences. Listen to their pronunciation.*

- I prefer to buy my **pro**duce in a fruit and vegetable store.
- The school has no **rec**ord of her. She's disappeared.
- You must have a **per**mit to park here.
- There is a **con**flict over who owns the land.

B Produce, record, permit *and* conflict *are verbs in these sentences. Listen to their pronunication.*

- They hope to pro**duce** new drugs.
- I always re**cord** my favorite TV programs and watch them on video later.
- The restaurant doesn't per**mit** smoking.
- What she said today con**flicts** with what she said yesterday.

C *Listen and underline the stressed syllable of each boldfaced word. Check your answers on page 79.*

1. You need a **permit** to march here.
2. There is a **conflict** among the members of the group.
3. The police won't **permit** us to stand there.
4. What was the **object** of the protest?
5. I can't go because the time **conflicts** with my job interview.
6. I **object** to what they say about us.

PROBLEM SOLVING

A *Read and listen to each problem. Choose a solution and write your reason for choosing that solution.*

Problem 1

Your friend wants to be an actress. She was offered the starring role in a movie, but the director says that in order to be in it, she must gain thirty pounds. She's of average weight now.

You advise her:

a. to take the part and gain the weight.

b. to give up the part because gaining so much weight is unhealthy.

c. to change the director's mind.

d. other: _____

Reason: _____

Problem 2

Eighty percent of people who have a certain gene get a bad disease. Only 10 percent of people without that gene get that disease. There is an an easy test to find out if you have the gene. Your family has a history of the disease.

You:

a. take the test to find out if you have the gene.

b. don't take the test for fear the results may be used against you.

c. don't take the test because you don't want to know.

d. other: _____

Reason: _____

Problem 3

You are a medical doctor. After a series of tests, you are almost certain that a middle-aged patient is suffering from the early stages of Alzheimer's disease.

You:

a. tell the patient what she has.

b. tell the patient's family and let them tell the patient.

c. don't tell the patient or the patient's family at this time. There's no cure and soon they will realize the truth.

d. other: _____

Reason: _____

Problem 4

You are a medical doctor. Your patient had a head injury. As a result, he developed epilepsy. Epilepsy is a disease of the brain that often causes a patient to have seizures in which the body moves in a violent, uncontrolled way. In your country there is a law that says you cannot drive a car until you are free of seizures for three years. Your patient is taking medication and has been free of seizures for six months. He has a new job that requires driving and he has resumed driving. You know that the job is important to your patient. However, you believe he is taking a chance by driving.

You:

a. report his driving to the government.

b. don't say anything and hope for the best.

c. try to convince your patient to stop driving and then report him if he doesn't listen.

d. other: _____

Reason: _____

B *Work in small groups. Talk about each problem in Part A and decide what your group would do.*

FROM THE NEWS

A *Answer the questions.*

1. About how many hours a night do you need to sleep?
2. How many hours do you get?
3. Do you prefer to wake up early or late?

Now read and listen to the article.

SLEEP-DEPRIVED TEENS RUN RISK OF DEPRESSION

It's 7:45 A.M. Don't expect a cheery "good morning" from Kami Obradovic.

"At that early hour I don't know my own name," said the sixteen-year-old student.

Like other teenagers, Obradovic gets less sleep time than the nine and one-quarter hours she should be getting. What she might not know is that this puts her at risk for depression, says Mary Carskadon, a professor and sleep specialist at Brown University Medical School in the United States.

The link between depression and insufficient sleep in teenagers pops up over and over in research, Carskadon says. What really bothers her is that teenagers actually know how much sleep they need. They just don't get any support to figure out how to get it.

Carskadon says that a good start might be schools starting no earlier than 8:30 A.M. But she doesn't expect that to happen.

"Sleep is the forgotten country in the modern world," she says. "It is scorned as a waste of time; a burden that gets in the way of both work and play."

For teenagers, bedtime becomes an issue of showing their independence. "I have yet to hear a teenager brag about how much sleep they had or how early they went to bed," says Carskadon.

Older teenagers are frequently driven to sleep deprivation by their ambitions, says Carskadon. Admission boards at colleges tell them they need high test scores, volunteer experience, and to be captain of a sports team for good measure. Sleep gets edged out.

B *Mark the following sentences* **T** *(true),* **F** *(false), or* **?** *(It doesn't say).*

_____ 1. Research has shown a relationship between depression and too much sleep.

_____ 2. Research has shown a relationship between depression and too little sleep.

_____ 3. Most teens don't need much sleep.

_____ 4. Most teens don't know what they need.

_____ 5. Not all people need the same amount of sleep.

_____ 6. Many people think sleep is a waste of time.

_____ 7. Many people think sleep is good for you.

WORDS AND PHRASES

A *Look at the words or phrases in the box. Find and circle them in the news article on page 76. Then write them next to their meaning.*

a waste of time	link	gets in the way of	support
~~sleep deprived~~	at risk	insufficient	

1. lacking sleep: ___sleep deprived___

2. in danger: _____

3. the connection: the _____

4. not enough: _____

5. help: _____

6. a foolish way to spend time: _____

7. interferes with: _____

B *Use the correct form of your answers from Part A to complete the sentences.*

1. There's a _____ between high cholesterol and heart disease.

2. Some people think doing exercise is _____, but most research shows that exercise is necessary for good health.

3. I'm _____. For the past week, I've been going to bed at midnight and getting up at five.

4. That water is okay to drink. You're not _____ of getting sick.

5. Many children think that sleep _____ having fun, so they don't want to go to bed at night.

6. We need your _____ in our fight against discrimination.

7. _____ sleep causes mistakes.

Act It Out

Act out the situation with a partner. Use the language from the box.

ASKING ABOUT A MEDICAL PROBLEM	DESCRIBING A MEDICAL PROBLEM
What seems to be the problem?	I have a *headache.* *stomachache.* *sore throat.*
How long have you had this problem?	I feel *dizzy.* *nauseous.* *tired all the time.*

SUGGESTING A REMEDY

Why don't you *rest for a few days?* *drink a lot of fluids?*

Have you tried *aspirin?* *taking vitamins?*

Situation

A: You are a doctor. **B** is your patient. Ask questions to find out what the problem is. Make suggestions.

B: You are sick and have gone to the doctor. Describe your problem and listen to your doctor's advice.

> EXAMPLE
>
> *Doctor:* Hello, Dan.
> *Patient:* Hi, Dr. Finkel.
> *Doctor:* Dan, how are you feeling?
> *Patient:* Not so good.
> *Doctor:* What seems to be the problem?
> *Patient:* I . . .

PROVERBS

Work in small groups. Discuss what these sayings mean and give real-life examples.

> ◆ *Laughter is the best medicine.*
>
> ◆ *Medicine is a science. The practice of medicine is an art.*
>
> ◆ *Many people call a doctor when all they want is an audience.*

BEYOND THE CLASSROOM

Many people are turning to alternative medicine such as herbs, massage, homeopathy, or acupuncture.

Work in small groups. Choose one type of alternative medicine to research. Report to the class the following information:

- Where does this type of alternative medicine come from?
- What problems does it help?
- Do you know anyone who has tried it? What were the results?

> **EXAMPLE**
>
> Shiatsu *is a Japanese word that translates as "finger pressure." However, people who do this form of massage use the palms of the hands, the forearms, elbows, knees, and feet, as well as the fingers and thumbs. Shiatsu can help a variety of problems including muscle and joint pain, headaches, migraines, stress, and insomnia. Miriam's grandfather has tried it . . .*

Answers to Pronunciation C, page 74:

1. per<u>mit</u>   4. <u>ob</u>ject

2. <u>con</u>flict   5. con<u>flicts</u>

3. per<u>mit</u>   6. <u>ob</u>ject

Money

THINK ABOUT THE TOPIC

1. How would suddenly having a huge amount of money change your life?
2. In what ways would it make your life better?
3. How might it make your life worse?

TALK ABOUT YOUR EXPERIENCE

A *Answer the questions. Then ask a classmate.*

	You	Your Classmate
1. When you were a child, how did you get money?		
2. When did you first earn money?		
3. In deciding on a career, how important is the salary? a. very important b. important c. not so important d. not important		
4. What would be the biggest change in your life if you suddenly lost all your money?		
5. What can't money buy?		

B *Discuss with the class.*

1. How many items did your class come up with for question 5? Do you all agree?

2. Do you think that your society places too much emphasis on material things? In what ways? Do you think that societies in the past were different? How?

LISTENING

A *Answer the questions before you listen.*

1. Do you have credit cards? How many?

2. What kinds of things do you buy with cash? What do you buy with your credit cards?

3. Is there an advantage to having a credit card? Explain.

B *Listen to the conversation and mark the following statements T (true) or F (false). Change the false statements to true ones.*

_____ **1.** Russ wants a CD player.

_____ **2.** The CD player is very expensive.

_____ **3.** Russ doesn't have a credit card.

_____ **4.** Russ has charged a lot of things on his credit card.

_____ **5.** The credit card company charges 10 percent interest.

_____ **6.** Russ is glad he got a credit card.

C *Discuss in small groups.*

1. What are the dangers of giving people credit cards?
2. At what age do you think people should get credit cards?

PRONUNCIATION

The intonation, or the way a sentence is spoken, can change the meaning of the sentence.

A *Listen to the conversations.*

1. A: Use your credit card.
   B: I can't.
2. A: You can't use a credit card.
   B: I can't?

In conversation **1** when B says, "I can't," he is making a statement. His voice goes down. In conversation **2**, when B says, "I can't," he is asking a question. His voice goes up.

B *Now listen to these sentences. Decide if the speaker is making a statement or asking a question. Add a period (.) or a question mark (?) at the end of each sentence. Check your answers on page 89.*

1. **a.** The company sends credit cards to teenagers_____
   b. The company sends credit cards to teenagers_____

2. **a.** You don't have any money_____
   b. You don't have any money_____

3. **a.** He gets offers all the time_____
   b. He gets offers all the time_____

4. **a.** This is a good price_____
   b. This is a good price_____

C *Work with a partner. Take turns saying the sentences from Pronunciation B as statements and as questions. Listen to your partner and decide whether he or she is making a statement or asking a question.*

PROBLEM SOLVING

A *Read and listen to each problem. Choose a solution and write your reason for choosing that solution.*

Problem 1

Your sister is in her second year of college, and she has to decide on a major. She loves to write poetry and says that when she finishes college, she wants to be a poet. Your father thinks she should get a teaching degree so that she will have a more financially secure job after college.

You:

a. agree with your father.

b. tell your sister to follow her dream.

c. send your sister to a counselor for advice.

d. other: _____

Reason: _____

Problem 2

A woman is writing her will. She has two married sons. Each son has two children. Her older son and his wife are very well-to-do and have always been good about saving money. Money burns a hole in the pockets of her younger son and his wife. The woman is worried that her grandchildren from her younger son will not have enough money for college. She therefore wants to leave her younger son more money than her older son.

You:

a. think she is wrong. She should leave them the same amount.

b. agree with the woman. Her older son doesn't need the money.

c. tell the woman to ask her older son to help his niece and nephew with college if they need the help.

d. other: _____

Reason: _____

(continued on next page)

Problem 3

Your friend is in her late thirties. She's about to get married for the first time. She and her fiancé both have had good jobs, but while she has saved money for the past fifteen years, her fiancé hasn't. She can't decide whether to keep the money she has earned in a separate account or open a joint account.

You advise her to:

a. open a joint account.

b. keep her money in a separate account and tell her fiancé.

c. keep her money in a separate account but not tell her fiancé.

d. other: _____

Reason: _____

Problem 4

Every year a number of students drop out of high school before graduating. In order to encourage these students to stay in school, the school administration decided to pay them money. To receive the money, the students must attend class five days in a row, come to school on time, do all their homework, and bring all necessary school supplies. To be in the program, students must have had problems in school in the past. Some people think that this will help keep these students in school. Others believe it is unfair to the majority of students who have never had problems.

You think that:

a. the administration found a good way to help students with problems.

b. the administration found a way of rewarding bad behavior.

c. the administration's idea is good, but it won't work.

d. other: _____

Reason: _____

B *Work in small groups. Talk about each problem in Part A and decide what your group would do.*

FROM THE NEWS

A *Answer the questions.*

1. Do you think parents should give their children pocket money?
2. Should children do chores for money?

Now read and listen to the article.

YOUNG SPENDERS

In Ireland, Saturday morning may be the day banks traditionally close, but if you are of school age, it's the day long associated with pocket money. The words *pocket money* seem to belong to the past, evoking images of china piggy banks and a simple selection of things to spend small amounts of money on. Do children still get pocket money, and if so, what do they spend it on?

Well, it would appear that a lot of children still do get the luxury of a small amount of money every week. Brother and sister Adam and Monique Kerroun live in Mullingar, Ireland. He is ten and she is seven years old.

"I get 2 pounds every week," Adam says. "I save a lot of it, and only spend 50 pence at most. I buy a drink, or sweets, or a few chips. I'm saving for a Playstation; everyone else in the class has one and I'm fed up with being left out of what they're talking about. Playstations cost around 100 pounds and I've saved 45 at least."

"Every 20 (pounds) I save, Mum or Dad give me 5 pounds," Adam explains.

"I don't really like only getting 2 pounds", he confides. "My friend gets 5 pounds every week, and he's only nine. I think 3 would be fairer." His sister, Monique, gets 1 pound. "Sometimes I save it when I'm in a good mood, and when I'm in a bad mood and my brother is annoying me, I go to the shop and spend it all! I buy little balls of chewing gum and lollipops."

Some of Monique's friends get pocket money and some don't. Like customers watching interest rates in banks, children do compare the amounts they get against what their friends get. "My friend Emma gets 10 (pounds)," she reveals, in awed tones. "But she buys good things for her mammy out of it, like flowers."

So what does psychologist Jane Fry, who specializes in working with young people, think of pocket money?

"We are a consumer society, a money society, so it's of great value for a child to have his or her own money. From a learning point of view, it's better to be given money in a lump sum so that you have to make it last, rather than think you can get a bit every day."

B *Use the information from the article to complete the chart.*

	Adam	Monique
Age		
Amount of pocket money		
What money is used for		
Attitude towards pocket money		

C *What does the psychologist think about giving young people pocket money? Do you agree?*

WORDS AND PHRASES

A *Find and underline these words and phrases in the article on page 85.*

evoking	luxury	left out of	save
in a bad mood	fairer	associated	

B *Find a word or phrase from the box that has the same meaning as the boldfaced words in the sentence. Write the word or phrase on the line. You may have to change the form of a verb to agree with the subject.*

_____evokes_____ 1. For me, Tahiti **brings forth** pictures of beautiful white beaches.

_____ 2. I always **made a connection between** summer and travel.

_____ 3. Though we'd love to take the trip, we can't afford the **needless expense** right now.

_____ 4. One of my friends spends all the money he earns. Another friend **puts** almost all of it **away for later**.

_____ 5. He wants to be in on all the games. Even though he's so young, he doesn't want to be **apart from** the action.

_____ **6.** I think it would be **more just** to give each child the same allowance.

_____ **7.** It's difficult to get him to smile. He is always **grumpy**.

ACT IT OUT

A *Read this story. Can you guess the ending? Check your answer on page 89.*

A long time ago a poor man wanted to give his king a present. The only thing the man had was a simple wooden bowl. The king had never seen such a bowl before. In appreciation and thanks, he gave the man a pot of gold.

Now the man was richer than he ever thought possible, and he became greedy.

He said to himself, "The king gave me a pot of gold for a simple wooden bowl. Imagine what he'll give me if I give him a golden chair."

So the man took the pot of gold and with it bought a golden chair. When the king got the golden chair, he said, "How can I repay this man? I have only one thing as precious as this chair."

B *Act out the situation with a partner. Use the language from the box.*

PRESENTING SOMEONE WITH SOMETHING	EXPRESSING THANKS
I'd like you to have this gift.	Thank you so very much.
I hope you like it.	It was so kind of you.
shirt.	Thanks. It's great.
I thought you'd like this *necklace.*	Thanks a lot. I love it.
book.	

Situation

A: It's your friend's birthday. Give him or her a gift.

B: It's your birthday. Thank your partner for the gift.

PROVERBS

A *Read these well-known proverbs.*

- ◆ *A penny saved is a penny earned.*

- ◆ *The love of money is the root of all evil.*

- ◆ *Money doesn't grow on trees.*

B *Work in small groups. Answer the questions.*

1. What do these proverbs mean?
2. Do you agree with any of them?
3. Give a situation in which someone might use each proverb.

BEYOND THE CLASSROOM

A *Work with a partner. Rank occupations from highest salary (1) to lowest salary (10) in the country you are in now. Then check the Internet or an almanac for the average salaries of the occupations. Write the average salary next to the occupation in the chart. Did you rank the salaries correctly?*

Occupation	Salary	Rank
primary school teacher		
lawyer		
professional baseball player		
doctor		
nurse		
actor		
plumber		
police officer		
CEO (chief executive officer) of a big corporation		
university professor		

B *Discuss with the class.*

1. Do you think any of these occupations are underpaid or overpaid? Why?
2. Are the rankings the same in other countries?

Sports

A

B

C

THINK ABOUT THE TOPIC

1. Have you ever tried rock climbing (A), inline skating (B), skydiving (C) or another extreme sport?
2. What would you say to a friend who wanted to try these sports?
3. In your opinion, is the thrill worth the possible danger? Why or why not?

TALK ABOUT YOUR EXPERIENCE

A *Answer the questions. Then ask a classmate.*

	You	Your Classmate
1. What's the most popular sport in your country?		
2. What sports do you like to play?		
3. What sports do you like to watch?		
4. Is keeping score very important for you or do you prefer playing without keeping score?		
5. Why do you play sports?		

B *Discuss with the class.*

• What are the different reasons people play sports (to win, to relax, to exercise)?

LISTENING

A *Answer the questions before you listen.*

• Do you think it's good for children and teens to join a competitive sports team? Why or why not?

B *Listen to the conversation and mark the following statements* T *(true)* or F *(false). Change the false statements to true ones.*

_____ **1.** Adam has a very bad cold.

_____ **2.** Adam's father doesn't want Adam to play baseball today.

_____ **3.** Adam doesn't want to go to the baseball game.

_____ **4.** Adam's mother thinks Adam should skip today's game.

_____ **5.** Adam's father used to play soccer.

_____ **6.** Adam and his father are a lot alike.

_____ **7.** Adam isn't a very good ball player.

_____ **8.** Adam is interested in sports.

C *Work with a partner. Discuss your answers to these questions. Give reasons.*

1. Do you think the father is wrong to push his son to play baseball?
2. If you were the mother, what would you say?

PRONUNCIATION

When *can* is followed by a verb, the stress is on the main verb. The vowel sound in *can* is short and unstressed: /kən/ or /kn/.

A *Listen to the example.*

• I can help you.

When *can't* is followed by a main verb, both *can't* and the main verb are stressed. The vowel sound in *can't* is longer and stressed: /kænt/.

B *Listen to the example.*

• I can't help you.

C *Listen and repeat these sentences. Pay attention to the pronunciation of* can *and* can't.

1. I can't play today.
2. You can't miss a game.
3. Maybe he can skip one game.
4. I can play tomorrow.

D *Work with a partner. Take turns saying either statement A or B. Your partner gives the correct response.*

Statement	**Response**
1. A: I can hear you.	Good.
B: I can't hear you.	I'll speak louder.
2. A: I can go to the game.	That's wonderful.
B: I can't go to the game.	I'm sorry to hear that.
3. A: I can catch well.	Good. We need a good catcher.
B: I can't catch well.	Don't worry. It doesn't matter.
4. A: I can see the ball.	Where is it?
B: I can't see the ball.	It's over there.

PROBLEM SOLVING

A *Read and listen to each problem. Choose a solution and write your reason for choosing that solution.*

Problem 1

You're on a soccer team. The team plays games every week. Your friend invited you to a concert that you would love to go to, but the concert is at the same time as your game.

You decide to:

a. miss the concert.

b. miss the soccer game.

c. go to the soccer game for a while. Then say you are sick and go to the concert.

d. other: _____

Reason: _____

Problem 2

Your friends' son is ten years old. He's overweight and not good at sports. However, where he lives almost every boy joins the baseball and soccer leagues. Last year he was alone on weekends because all the other children were busy with their teams. Your friends ask for your advice.

You tell them to:

a. encourage their son to join a sports team. If he's on a winning team, he'll enjoy the game even if he isn't a good player.

b. discourage him from joining a sports team. Children can be mean and he'll feel hurt.

c. find other activities that he's good at.

d. other: _____

Reason: _____

(continued on next page)

Sports   93

Problem 3

Your fourteen-year-old brother loves sports. He's a bright boy but a poor student. Last year he was a star player on the basketball team, but his school grades were terrible. This year he wants to join the team again. Your mother thinks he should study more and forget about basketball. Your father thinks he should be allowed to join the team but get extra help with his schoolwork. They ask for your opinion.

You:

a. agree with your mother because when he practices basketball, he's too tired to study.

b. agree with your father because your brother loves the game, and being on a team teaches him about sportsmanship and discipline.

c. say that you don't want to take sides.

d. other: _____

Reason: _____

B *Work in small groups. Talk about each problem in Part A and decide what your group would do.*

FROM THE NEWS

A *Answer the questions.*

1. Should sports rules be changed to accommodate people with physical disabilities? For example, should a golfer who can't walk long distances be allowed to use a golf cart?

2. Should sports allow for people with mental disabilities? For example, if a person can't keep score, could another keep score for this person? Why or why not?

Now read and listen to the article.

HELPING YOUNG GOLFER WITH TRUE HANDICAP

The United States Supreme Court recently ruled that golfer Casey Martin, who suffers from a medical problem that makes walking difficult, can use a cart during professional golf tournaments.

Some say allowing Martin to ride between shots, instead of walk, as professional golfers do, gives him an unfair advantage. And walking, they say, is as much a part of the game as shot-making. But the Court disagreed. Justice John Paul Stevens said that "shot-making" is the heart of the game and that the Americans with Disabilities Act requires that facilities provide access to the disabled.

A somewhat similar case is developing in Zephyrhills, Florida. There, a young golfer with a mental handicap wants to play in the Greater Tampa Junior Golf Association tournaments. Matthew Ross is nine and suffers from autism, a disorder of the brain that causes a number of complications, including mental retardation and problems in social interaction and communication.

Matthew can walk, carry his bag, pick his clubs, tee the ball, and strike it. He also knows some of the game's rules, including what to do when he hits a ball out of play.

The problem is he can't keep score. His brain will not allow it. And under the rules of the Greater Tampa Junior Golf Association, Matthew must be able to keep his score, as well as that of other players, to participate. Matthew's mother, Susan, would like to keep score when he plays. It is a simple request, one that should be granted. It would not give Matthew an unfair advantage. It would just put him on an even par with the other children who do not suffer his handicap.

B *Circle the best answer to complete the sentences according to the article.*

1. This article _____.
   a. gives the opinion of the writer
   b. tells a folktale
   c. reports an event

2. The author of this article _____.
   a. disagrees with the United States Supreme Court ruling
   b. agrees with the United States Supreme Court ruling
   c. doesn't tell you whether or not he agrees with the United States Supreme Court ruling

(continued on next page)

3. The writer believes _____.

   a. rules must be followed to the letter

   b. there are occasions when rules should be changed

   c. people with handicaps should not play against people without handicaps

WORDS AND PHRASES

A *Find the phrase from the box with the same meaning as the boldfaced word(s) in the sentence. Write the phrase on the line next to the sentence.*

should be granted	taking place	an unfair advantage
recently ruled	an even par	keep score

_____ 1. Our school district **just voted** that all athletes must have at least a B average to play on school teams.

_____ 2. We think that rule gives one side **more chances to win**.

_____ 3. Many different events are **happening** at the same time.

_____ 4. Who's going to **count the points** to see who's winning?

_____ 5. Now they are starting off on **the same level**.

_____ 6. What they ask for **ought to be given**.

B *Do you understand these sports idioms? Complete the sentences with idioms from the box. Part of the idiom may already be in the sentence.*

have a ball	whole new ball game	start the ball rolling
I'm game	touch base	cover all the bases

1. Our business is a whole _____ now that there's a competitor on the same street.

2. We need to discuss several items at this meeting. Mary, would you _____ rolling.

3. We've got a lot of people working on each part of the project. We want to _____ bases.

4. We haven't spoken in a while. I'm calling to _____ and make sure the project is going well.

5. I'm so excited about my vacation. Six of us are going hiking and camping. I'm sure we'll have _____.

6. Planning a surprise party for Joe will be a lot of work, but _____ if you are.

C *Match the idioms on the left with their definitions on the right. Write the letter on the line.*

_____ 1. have a ball   **a.** I'm willing

_____ 2. whole new ball game   **b.** get things started

_____ 3. I'm game   **c.** have fun

_____ 4. touch base   **d.** make contact

_____ 5. start the ball rolling   **e.** to deal with a situation thoroughly

_____ 6. cover all the bases   **f.** a new situation

ACT IT OUT

Act out the situation on the next page with a partner. Use the language from the box.

GIVING INSTRUCTIONS	CLARIFYING INSTRUCTIONS
Hold the *bat / racquet / ball / club* like this.	Like this?
	Is this what you mean?
Stand in this position.	Do you mean this way?
Lean forward.	
Bend your *knees. / elbows.*	

Situation

A coach (**A**) is giving a first-time player (**B**) a sports lesson.

A: You're a sports coach. Choose a sport. Show a first-time player how to do some aspect of the sport, for example, how to serve the ball in tennis, how to hit the ball in baseball, or how to shoot a basket in basketball.

B: You're a first-time player. Ask your coach to clarify his or her instructions.

> **EXAMPLE**
>
> A: *Have you ever played tennis?*
> B: *No.*
> A: *Well, I'd like to show you how to serve.*
> B: *OK.*
> A: *Are you right- or left-handed?*
> B: *Right-handed.*
> A: *Then hold the racquet in your right hand. Put your feet about a foot apart and bend your knees.*
> B: *Like this?*
> A: *Not exactly. More like this. Your hand should go around the leather handle.*
> B: *Oh.*

PROVERBS

Work in small groups. Discuss what these sayings mean. Do you agree or disagree? Why?

> ◆ *It's not whether you win or lose; it's how you play the game.*
>
> ◆ *No pain, no gain.*
>
> ◆ *Winning isn't everything, but losing isn't anything.*

BEYOND THE CLASSROOM

A *Make teams of four or five students. Check the Internet or reference books for information about these athletes. Take notes on important facts.*

1. Mohammed Ali
2. Sergei Bubka
3. Wayne Gretsky
4. Michael Jordan
5. Konishiki
6. Jesse Owens
7. Pelé
8. Monica Seles
9. Naoko Takahashi
10. Venus Williams
11. Tiger Woods

Each team uses its notes to play this game against the other teams. Decide on a time limit.

1. Give a fact about one of these athletes. Do not say the person's name.

2. Students on other teams raise their hands as soon as they know who the fact is about.

3. The first to give the correct answer wins a point for his or her team. A wrong answer loses a point.

> **EXAMPLE**
>
> A: In the 2000 Olympics, this woman won the marathon.
> B: Naoko Takahashi.
> A: Right. You get a point.

Pets

THINK ABOUT THE TOPIC

1. What are some practical reasons why people have pets?

2. What are other reasons for having pets?

TALK ABOUT YOUR EXPERIENCE

A *Answer the questions. Then ask a classmate. Check (✓) Yes or No.*

	You		Your Classmate	
	Yes	No	Yes	No
1. Have you ever had a pet? If you had a pet:				
a. did you give it a name?	☐	☐	☐	☐
b. did you buy it special food?	☐	☐	☐	☐
c. did you talk to it?	☐	☐	☐	☐
d. did you teach it to do anything special?	☐	☐	☐	☐
2. If you've never had a pet:				
a. did you ever want one?	☐	☐	☐	☐
b. would you want one in the future?	☐	☐	☐	☐
3. Do you think it's good for children to have pets?	☐	☐	☐	☐
4. Do you think it's good for older people to have pets?	☐	☐	☐	☐

B *Discuss with the class.*

1. What is the most popular pet in your country? The second most popular pet?
2. What are the advantages of owning a pet?
3. What are the disadvantages of owning a pet?

LISTENING

A *Answer the questions before you listen.*

1. Have you ever lived in a place where pets were not allowed?
2. Do you think it's fair to exclude pets from an apartment building? Explain.
3. What do people do with their pets when they don't want them anymore or can't keep them?

B *Listen to the conversation and mark the following statements* T *(true)* or F *(false). Change the false statements to true ones.*

_____ **1.** The woman wants a two-bedroom apartment.

_____ **2.** The woman finds an apartment from an ad in the paper.

_____ **3.** The apartment is far from shopping.

_____ **4.** Apartments are easy to find at this time.

_____ **5.** The landlord doesn't allow pets in her apartments.

_____ **6.** Biddy is the name of the woman's pet.

_____ **7.** The man wants to take care of Biddy.

PRONUNCIATION

The following pairs of words begin and end with the same sound, but their vowels are different. People can easily confuse these words if the vowels are not pronounced carefully.

A *Listen and repeat each word pair.*

walk   work   won't   want

B *Listen as the speaker reads the sentences. Number the sentences in the order you hear them. Check your answers on page 108.*

_____ **a.** I walk to work.   _____ **d.** I want to work.

_____ **b.** I won't work.   _____ **e.** I want to walk.

_____ **c.** I won't walk.

C *Work with a partner. Take turns reading a statement from the left column. Your partner gives the correct response from the right column. Match the correct responses to their statements. Check your answers on page 108.*

Statements	*Responses*
_____ **1.** I walk to work.	**a.** Me, too. I enjoy working.
_____ **2.** I won't work.	**b.** Oh? I want to take the bus.
_____ **3.** I won't walk.	**c.** I won't walk either.
_____ **4.** I want to work.	**d.** I can't. My job is too far away.
_____ **5.** I want to walk.	**e.** Don't you need the money?

PROBLEM SOLVING

A *Read and listen to each problem. Choose a solution and write your reason for choosing that solution.*

Problem 1

You and your sweetheart are in love. You've been talking about marriage. Your sweetheart has a big, ugly, mean dog that you can't stand. Your sweetheart wants to keep the dog after you get married.

You:

a. find a new sweetheart.

b. hope to live longer than the dog.

c. learn to love the dog.

d. other: _____

Reason: _____

Problem 2

Your brother wanted a dog very much. Your mother got him a dog but agreed to keep the dog only as long as he took care of it. At first he did, but now, after three months, he only walks and feeds the dog after your mother reminds him several times.

You think she should:

a. keep on reminding him. After all, he does the work when reminded.

b. take care of the dog herself. She bought the dog, and she knows how careless your brother is.

c. give the dog away. Your brother must learn to be responsible.

d. other: _____

Reason: _____

Problem 3

A drug company has hired scientists to find a cure for a disease. The scientists are experimenting with monkeys. A group of citizens are protesting. They say the scientists are hurting and even killing monkeys in the experiments. They want the scientists to stop using live animals. The drug company says this is the only way to find a cure for the disease.

You are:

a. in favor of the experiments because humans are more important than animals.

b. against the experiments because animals don't have a choice and can't complain.

c. in favor of the experiments only if the animals are treated better.

d. other: _____

Reason: _____

B *Work in small groups. Talk about each problem in Part A and decide what your group would do.*

FROM THE NEWS

A *Answer the question.*

- A "guardian" is someone who is legally responsible for someone else. What's the difference between a "guardian" and an "owner"?

Now read and listen to the news from an online Web page about pets.

SAN FRANCISCO CITIZENS TO BECOME "PET GUARDIANS"

The Animal Control and Welfare Commission of San Francisco recently voted to call citizens with animal companions "pet guardians" as well as "pet owners" in official documents.

The Board of Supervisors has yet to approve the vote. Under California law, pets are considered personal property and supporters say the term "pet guardian" evokes warmth and compassion for pets and encourages people to adopt animals from shelters.

The majority of people at the commission's meeting were in favor of the term. However, there were a few in the crowd who voiced their opposition.

Pet owner Florence Sarrett said the change will make San Francisco a laughingstock. "My dog is my dog, just as my children are my children," she said.

San Francisco has one of the most unique animal shelters in the nation: a $7 million facility where stray cats and dogs live in private "condos" furnished with wicker furniture, pillows, framed prints, and TVs that play nature programs and cartoons.

Adapted from http://critterchatter.com

B *Mark the following sentences **T** (true) or **F** (false). Change the false statements to true ones.*

_____ **1.** People in the Animal Control and Welfare Commission of San Francisco think the expression "pet guardian" sounds warmer than the expression "pet owner."

_____ **2.** At this time, pets are not considered to be the property of their owners.

_____ **3.** At this time, official documents call people with animal companions "pet owners."

_____ **4.** Florence Sarrett thinks the new term is a good idea.

_____ **5.** If you are a laughingstock, it means everyone will laugh at you.

_____ **6.** The animal shelter in San Francisco is ordinary.

C *Discuss this comment with your class. Do you agree? Explain.*

- As long as there are homeless people, it is wrong to build $7 million shelters for stray cats and dogs. Animals should always come after people.

WORDS AND PHRASES

A *Match the name of the animal to its picture.*

| bird | mule | peacock | mouse | pig | owl |

1

2

3

4

5

6

B *Complete the sentences. Use the pictures in Part A to help you.*

1. She never says a word. She's as quiet as a ___mouse___.
2. She hardly eats at all. She eats like a _____.
3. He'll never change his mind. He's as stubborn as a _____.
4. What a messy eater! He eats like a _____.
5. He always gives good advice. He's as wise as an _____.
6. He thinks he's so wonderful. He's as proud as a _____.

C *Discuss with a partner.*

1. The sentences in Part B include common expressions about animals. Why do you think the animals have these associations? For example, are mice really quiet?
2. What kinds of associations do these animals have in different cultures?

ACT IT OUT

Act out the situation with a partner. Use the language from the box.

RAISING OBJECTIONS

	dog		walk it.
If we get a	bird	we'll have to	clean its cage.
	cat		feed it.

	dogs		cost a lot of money.
The problem with	birds	is they	make a big mess.
	cats		are difficult to train.

COUNTERING OBJECTIONS

	walking the dog in the rain.
I don't mind	cleaning the cage.
	feeding the cat.

	walk the dog.
It won't bother me to	clean the cage.
	feed the cat.

Situation

A: You want to get a pet. Try to persuade your roommate to agree.

B: You don't want to get a pet. Try to talk your roommate out of the idea.

EXAMPLE

A: *Look at that adorable puppy.*
  Let's bring it home.

B: *A puppy is a lot of work. We'll have to walk it in the rain.*

A: *I don't mind walking the dog in the rain.*

PROVERBS AND SAYINGS

A *Work with a partner. Complete the proverbs and sayings with the words from the box. Check your answers on page 108.*

cat	dog	bird (s)

1. The early _____ catches the worm.
2. A _____ has nine lives.
3. _____ is man's best friend.
4. Curiosity killed the _____.
5. It's a _____ eat _____ world.
6. _____ of a feather flock together.

B *Discuss the meaning of the proverbs and sayings in Part A with your classmates. Are there any sayings about dogs, cats, or birds in your language? Share them with the class.*

BEYOND THE CLASSROOM

Choose an unusual pet. Do research in books, on the Internet, or at a pet store. Find out what you need to do to take care of this pet. Report your findings to the class. Answer the questions in your report.

1. Food: What do you feed it? How often? How much?
2. Habitat: Where is it most comfortable?
3. Independence: How long can you leave it alone for?
4. Longevity: How long does this type of animal usually live?

Answers to Pronunciation B, page 102:

a. 3	d. 1
b. 2	e. 4
c. 5	

Answers to Pronunciation C, page 102:

1. d	4. a
2. e	5. b
3. c	

Answers to Proverbs A, page 107:

1. bird	4. cat
2. cat	5. dog, dog
3. Dog	6. Birds

The Right Gift

THINK ABOUT THE TOPIC

1. What's happening in the pictures?
2. How are the people in each picture related to each other?
3. How do the people feel about their gifts?

TALK ABOUT YOUR EXPERIENCE

A *Read the question and circle the letter of your answer. Then ask a classmate.*

1. About how many gifts do you buy in a year?
   a. less than five
   b. between five and ten
   c. between ten and thirty
   d. more than thirty

2. On what occasions do you give gifts?
   a. birthdays
   b. weddings
   c. anniversaries
   d. graduations
   e. religious holidays
   f. births
   g. visits
   h. other: _____

3. Who do you buy gifts for?
   a. family
   b. friends
   c. people who do things for you (for example, the mail carrier)

4. Which kinds of gifts do you not like to give? Which do you not like to receive? Why not?
   a. books
   b. clothes
   c. tickets to concerts, plays, or sports events
   d. games
   e. sports equipment
   f. electronic equipment
   g. leather items (wallets, belts)
   h. toys
   i. jewelry
   j. money
   k. flowers
   l. chocolates
   m. handmade gifts
   n. other: _____

LISTENING

A *Answer the questions before you listen.*

- Have you ever received a gift that you didn't want? What was the gift? What did you do with it?

B *Listen to the conversation. Then listen again and mark the following sentences* **T** *(true) or* **F** *(false).*

_____ **1.** Joan bought her sister-in-law and brother-in-law a box of chocolates.

_____ **2.** Joan brought her sister-in-law and brother-in-law a box of chocolates.

_____ **3.** Joan's co-workers gave her a box of chocolates.

_____ **4.** Joan's sister-in-law and brother-in-law don't like chocolate.

_____ **5.** Joan was surprised to see a card in the box of chocolates.

PRONUNCIATION

Usually the words with the most important meaning in a sentence are stressed. Stressing different words can change the meaning of the sentence.

A *Listen to the conversations.*

1. A: **I'm** finishing the dishes.
   B: Oh. I thought your brother was.

2. A: I'm finishing the **dishes**.
   B: Oh. I thought you were finishing the laundry.

3. A: I'm **finishing** the dishes.
   B: Oh. I thought you were starting them.

B *Work with a partner. The boldfaced words are stressed. Match the sentences in Column A with the appropriate responses in Column B. Write the letter on the line. Then take turns saying and responding to the sentences. Check your answers on page 118.*

A	B
_____ **1.** My aunt brought them **last** week.	**a.** I thought she baked them.
_____ **2.** My **aunt** brought them last week.	**b.** I thought it was the week before.
_____ **3.** My aunt **bought** them last week.	**c.** I thought it was your sister.

PROBLEM SOLVING

🎧 **A** *Read and listen to each problem. Choose a solution and write your reason for choosing that solution.*

Problem 1

You are invited to two weddings. One wedding will be a formal wedding and will cost a lot of money. The other wedding will be a simple, inexpensive party. You are equally close to both friends, and both families are neither rich nor poor.

You:

a. give both friends gifts that cost the same.

b. give the friend who is having the more expensive wedding a more expensive gift.

c. give gifts according to what you think each friend would want and don't worry about the cost.

d. other: _____

Reason: _____

Problem 2

For three years in a row, a friend has given you a bottle of cologne. It's always the same cologne, and you don't like the scent. You have always thanked your friend for the gift, so your friend has no idea that you don't really like it. It's coming to that time of year again.

You:

a. accept another bottle of cologne.

b. tell your friend that you've become allergic to it.

c. tell your friend that you'd prefer another cologne.

d. other: _____

Reason: _____

Your friend loves to give and receive gifts. She always reminds you of her birthday and holidays. You don't like the gifts she gives you. Either she gives you a cheap gift, beautifully wrapped in a box from an expensive store, or she gives you a second-hand gift. Once she gave you some earrings that she had worn the previous day. Last year you told her you'd rather not exchange gifts anymore, but she said she will give you a gift even if you don't give her one. What do you do?

You:

a. don't give her a gift.

b. give her a nice gift.

c. give her a cheap gift.

d. other: _____

Reason: _____

Your friend is an artist who gave you one of his paintings for your birthday. You never liked the painting and never hung it up. He is going to visit you next week. What will you do?

a. Hang his painting on the wall before he visits. Remove it when he leaves.

b. Nothing. Don't hang the painting up if you don't like it.

c. Hang it on the wall in an inconspicuous place and keep it there.

d. other: _____

Reason: _____

B *Work in small groups. Talk about each problem in Part A and decide what your group would do.*

A *Answer the questions.*

1. Have you ever given or received an inappropriate gift?
2. In what ways is gift giving different in different parts of the world?

Now read and listen to the article.

GIVING GIFTS AROUND THE WORLD

A well-chosen present can strengthen any friendship. But when giving gifts to people in other countries, you should know that it's not always just the thought that counts. In some places, the way you give is even more important than the gift. There are many similarities in gift giving, but customs differ from country to country, and the same item can give very different messages. Here's a quick look at gift giving around the world.

European cultures are similar to the cultures of the United States and Canada in many ways, but proper manners and protocol are even more important there than in the United States and Canada. Across Europe, a good gift is always a thoughtful one, appropriate to the relationship. Gifts should be tasteful and well chosen but not overly expensive.

When visiting a home, flowers are usually appreciated. However, chrysanthemums are a symbol of mourning in France, while in Germany red roses are reserved for lovers. European gifts tend to be simply but tastefully wrapped, and it's a nice idea to include a card with a handwritten note.

Gifts in Japan are seldom opened when given but are opened later in private. Never make a ceremony of the presentation, but take time to think about the way the gift is packaged. Gift wrapping is very important; rice paper signifies good taste, while ribbons and bows may not. Also remember never to give anyone a set of four. Four is considered bad luck.

In China as in Japan, gifts are usually exchanged in private, except during grand banquets. If you write a card, don't do it in red ink, which means you're cutting off a friendship. Finally, never give a watch or clock as a present, since the English word *clock* sounds like the Chinese word for *funeral*.

In Arab countries, gifts are also important, but there what counts most is the gift itself, rather than how it is wrapped or given. Generosity is appreciated by Arabs, so their gift giving tends to be very generous or not at all. Gifts are generally given in public and always offered with the right hand. Liquor is, of course, taboo. Also avoid artwork and other items with pictures of animals, many of which mean bad luck.

When giving gifts in Latin America, remember that Latin Americans tend to be giving people who always appreciate thoughtfulness. Good gifts need not be expensive as much as well chosen to recognize the tastes and interests of the one who is getting the gift. Business gifts in Latin America aren't generally exchanged until a personal relationship has developed or negotiations are over. Avoid gifts with company logos and never give knives, handkerchiefs, or anything colored black, purple, or associated with the number thirteen. A small token gift is always in order when you visit someone's home—for a wife, perfume, candy, flowers, or a kitchen item, and for the kids, the latest toy. A final caution for women in Latin America: Be especially aware of the possible misunderstanding giving a gift to a man may create.

B *Write the country or part of the world next to the sentence that describes its gift-giving customs according to the article.*

China	Arab countries	Latin America	France	Germany

_____ 1. A beautiful purple handkerchief would not be appreciated.

_____ 2. You wouldn't bring chrysanthemums if you are invited here for dinner.

_____ 3. You wouldn't bring a picture of a dog.

_____ 4. You wouldn't bring red roses when invited to your boss's home.

_____ 5. You wouldn't give your friend a clock.

C *Work in groups. Discuss the questions.*

1. How would you describe the gift-giving habits of your country? Are these habits different for different age groups? Explain.

2. What's most important for you when you give or receive a gift? What's not important?

3. When we say, "It's the thought that counts," what do we usually mean?

4. Do you know the gift-giving customs in any of the countries in the article? If so, do you agree with the author?

WORDS AND PHRASES

A *Read the words in the box. Write them next to their opposite meaning.*

inappropriate	generous	well-chosen	token	thoughtful

1. a cheap gift—a _____ gift

2. an appropriate gift—an _____ gift

3. a lavish gift—a _____ gift

4. a thoughtless gift—a _____ gift

5. a poorly chosen gift—a _____ gift

B *Work with a partner. Choose a gift for each person below. Then use a word from Part A to describe the gift for that person. Talk about these gifts with your partner.*

Person	**Gift**
grandparent	inline skates
son or daughter	new car
parent	magazine subscription
co-worker	gold watch
husband or wife	calendar
	box of chocolates

EXAMPLE

grandparent, a magazine subscription

A: *I think a magazine subscription is a thoughtful gift for a grandparent.*
B: *I agree. My grandma would love a gardening magazine.*

ACT IT OUT

Act out the situation with a partner. Use the language from the box.

MAKING SUGGESTIONS	REJECTING SUGGESTIONS
Why don't you get him a . . .? How about a . . .?	This shirt has too many *colors.* *buttons.* It's too *expensive* *small.* *plain.* This jacket *is too heavy.* *isn't warm enough.* *isn't big enough.*

Situation

A is looking at a catalog with **B**, trying to choose a birthday gift for someone.

A: You want to buy something that is nice for someone who is hard to please.

B: You are trying to help **A** choose a gift for someone who is hard to please.

> **EXAMPLE**
>
> *A: I'm having a tough time getting a gift for my dad.*
> *B: How about this silk shirt?*
> *A: It's too expensive. And it has too many colors.*
> *B: Well, this is a nice tie.*
> *A: It's much too bright.*
> *B: Well. Here's a nice umbrella.*
> *A: It's not big enough. He always uses big umbrellas.*

PROVERBS

Work in small groups. Discuss what these sayings mean.

- *Don't look a gift horse in the mouth.*

- *It is better to give than to receive.*

- *Give a man a fish and you feed him for a day.*
  Teach a man to fish and you feed him for life.

BEYOND THE CLASSROOM

Work in small groups. Bring in catalogs from different stores. Use the catalogs to choose gifts for the classmates in your group. Explain your gift choices to your group members.

> **EXAMPLE**
>
> *This coffeemaker would be a good gift for Pablo. It has a timer, so his coffee could be ready when he wakes up in the morning. This would save him time so he wouldn't be late for class.*

Answers to Pronunciation B, page 111:

1. b

2. c

3. a

APPENDIX

WORDS AND PHRASES

SOCIAL LANGUAGE/FUNCTIONS